What people are saying about *Shadow Work*:

This work confronts us as individuals and as organizational communities with the shadow of our existence. Although a look at our shadow (whether individually or corporately) can be painful, Dr. Ruth does not leave us there but offers hope for healing and wholeness in our relationships and our lives that we all so desperately seek. This book will push the reader to deal with the fears that beset us, and to hopefully emerge a little wiser in how to live out grace and healing in all of life's relationships. To say that this book moved me lacks the power in truly describing its impact. It radically changed how I think about myself and my world and enabled me to rethink the power of healing in confronting the shadow.

Jonathan D. Rohrer, Ph.D.
College of Osteopathic Medicine
Michigan State University

Finally, here is a book, lucid and well-written, that bridges the worlds of Christianity and psychology without denigrating either. Further, by examining the shadow of the church, this book speaks courageously to the confusion and disillusionment which has caused many to leave organized religion. After reading *Shadow Work*, I suspect not a few of these same people will return to the church, equipped to help make it the living community it is intended to be.

Elizabeth Austin, Ph.D.
Psychologist

Dr. Ruth presents a unique and effective look into the role of spiritual dynamics in reaching human wholeness.

Henry Lazenby, Ph.D.
Theologian and writer

SHADOW WORK

A New Guide to Spiritual and Psychological Growth

Dr. Michael Ruth

Growth Solutions
KNOXVILLE, TN

First printing 1999

ISBN 0-9668083-5-5

LCCN 99-71757

ATTENTION CORPORATIONS, UNIVERSITIES, COLLEGES, AND PROFESSIONAL ORGANIZATIONS: Quantity discounts are available on bulk purchases of this book for educational purposes. Special books or book excerpts can also be created to fit specific needs. For information, please contact Growth Solutions, P.O. Box 32805, Knoxville, TN 37930-2805.

Acknowledgments

I would like to express my gratitude to the following individuals for their contributions to this work: Thank you Scotty, for your assistance, advice, and feedback on the manuscript. Thank you Liz; your friendship, and your enthusiasm for this project has meant more than I can say. And thank you Jonathan and Jennifer; your behind the scenes support helped bring this book to reality.

The author gratefully acknowledges permission to quote from the following:

Scripture taken from the Holy Bible, New International Version®. Copyright ©1973, 1978, 1984 by International Bible Society. Used by permission of Zondervan Publishing House. All rights reserved. The "NIV" and New International Version" trademarks are registered in the United States Patent and Trademark Office by International Bible Society. Use of either trademark requires the permission of International Bible Society.

Scripture quotations from THE MESSAGE. Copyright © by Eugene H. Peterson 1993, 1994, 1995. Used by permission of NavPress Publishing Group.

Excerpt from "As I Walked Out One Evening" in Auden: Poems, selected by Edward Mendelson, copy-

*The names and identifying data of the individuals referred
to in this book have been changed to protect their privacy
and confidentiality.*

For Susan.
This, the first, and all to follow.

Contents

Introduction

This is a book of hope and healing. It is about recovering our dignity as human beings—about restoring our lives to the wholeness which is our birthright. We have both lost and abandoned the honorable station to which we were created and called. This is undeniable. Our society will no longer allow us to look at ourselves and draw any other conclusion. It is clear that modern man, as Jung says, is in search of a soul. It is time we made a return—a return to our true Self. The following chapters attempt to show us how to do just that.

I want to persuade the reader of these pages to realize that something is wrong, that we are living far below what it means to be human, but that the problem, though serious, is a correctable one. I want to be persuasive regarding our call to psychospiritual wholeness—what I call the walk of life. I hope to enlarge our understanding of the walk of life and to suggest how we may begin and then progress down that long and winding road.[1]

---

[1] I should say a word about my use of the masculine pronoun in reference to God throughout this book. I am aware that some may view this as thoughtless and sexist. It is neither. Throughout the book I have deliberately avoided the sexist tone. Speaking here as a Christian theologian, there is scant textual justification for referring to God as female. He has revealed himself as male throughout both Testaments of the Bible. Further, in the New Testament the church is referred to as the *bride* of Christ. Having said this, I would quickly add that I believe God is androgynous in the sense that in his person he is the perfect expression of those personality characteristics which we as a society have arbitrarily and artificially divided into masculine or feminine.

To use a medical metaphor, parts one and two of the book are diagnostic in nature. They tell us what is wrong. They tell us why things are as they are. Knowledge is power; if we do not know what is wrong, and why, it is very unlikely that we can do anything about the problem. Thankfully, we are not in ignorance here.

I say that this is a book of hope, but part one may seem to belie that fact. This portion of the book is like the report given by a physician who has just discovered a malignant tumor in your body. It is not pleasant to listen to, but it is essential. The good news is that the tumor threatening us—both as individuals and as a society at large—need not be terminal. Unlike cancers that ravage the body, it is our choice as to whether or not this tumor spreads. Again, I am back to the subject of healing.

As I say in the initial section, we know what our problem is. The tumor of our soul—both individual and collective—has been recognized and isolated. Thanks to assistance from an ancient text (which enlightens our understanding of spiritual darkness) and the psychology of C. G. Jung (which expands on this "shadow" of our nature) we know what the problem is. Together, they help us understand our predicament.

Part two examines the shadow-side of our existence both individually and collectively or organizationally. The organization I have chosen to scrutinize is the church.

There is a good deal of essential preliminary information required before one studies the church in terms of its collective shadow. This presented a problem as far as the organization and structure of this book is concerned. To put the material in the body of the book did not quite work because, though integral to the subject, it does not relate directly to the issue of shadow. The way I have chosen around this problem is that of placing the material in appendix (see *Understanding the Church*).

To continue with the medical metaphor, beyond part two, the remainder of the book is prescriptive, which is to say it is occupied with the subject of treatment. Thankfully, our condition need not be a sickness unto death. Sections three and four look at what it means to confront the shadow and just how we are to accomplish this. We do this as we learn to fight the good fight (part three) and as we practice redemptive community (part four). Parts five and six close the book with an in-depth look at the vocation to which each of us is called—our psychospiritual development. As I have said, my own term for this, the essential and primary calling we all share, is *the walk of life*.

I return on final time to our medical metaphor. If, after having heard the diagnosis, we commit ourselves to the prescribed treatment, the prognosis for our recovery is not only good—it is excellent! In fact we will find ourselves in better health than we ever imagined possible.

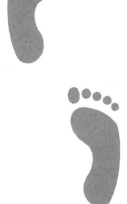

Part One

THE DYING OF THE LIGHT

The shadow of one dark wing
is over all Tellus.[1]
—C. S. Lewis

CHAPTER 1

Utopia or Dystopia?

Woody Allen says, "More than at any other time in history, mankind faces a crossroads. One path leads to despair and utter hopelessness. The other, to total extinction. Let us pray we have the wisdom to choose correctly."[2] In his whimsical style Allen has put his finger on a fact. Something is wrong with us. And while things are certainly not as bleak as the famous satirist quips, they are bad.

At the birth of the twentieth century the Western world was positively giddy with anticipation over the coming utopia. After all, humanity was getting better and better—so the argument went. The Golden Age was dawning. Human potential seemed limitless. Education would free us from our moral defects as the miracles of medicine would liberate us from our physical infirmities. The enemies which had long plagued the world—disease, violence, ignorance, warfare—would fade away. Paradise would be achieved. Humanity would celebrate the new utopia. Uh-huh.

---

[1] C. S. Lewis, *That Hideous Strength* (The Macmillan Company, 1946), 293.

[2] Foster Hirsch, *Love, Sex, Death and the Meaning of Life* (McGraw Hill, 1981), 92.

An economic depression, a couple of world wars, and a few "police actions" later and the world is a bit more sober, even jaded. You couldn't find a classic utopian today with a pair of bloodhounds. To the contrary, we seem to be headed not for utopia but dystopia. What change in our collective spirit fuels this social entropy? Just what is behind all of this?

On many occasions I have heard my father talk about his experiences during the days of the Great Depression (although he always said he could never figure out what was so great about it!). He grew up in rural Eastern Kentucky and life was as hard and jagged as the mountains of that area—a hardship made even worse by the Depression. Despite the tough times there was a general morality, a code of ethics that people adhered to. There was a sense of community. As I have heard my father put it so many times, "People didn't even lock their doors; they didn't lock their smokehouses." There was simply no worry that people, even hungry people, would steal from you. That was only one generation ago.

Contrast this with what happened just a few years back when one of our major cities experienced a power blackout. Looting was rampant. Vandalism, destruction for destruction's sake, occurred throughout the city. Today, even the winning of a sports championship provides all the motivation necessary for a city to erupt into plundering and destruction.

Take another example. A recent news magazine[1] dealing with violence in the public schools included a picture of designer jackets for elementary students. The thing that made these jackets unique is the fact that they are, in actuality, bullet-proof vests. These vests are designed to keep the children safe while they are in school and walking through the

---

[1] *U. S. News & World Report*, 8 November 1993.

neighborhood. This is not just a matter of parental paranoia. On any given day, upwards of one-half million high school students carry guns to school. The neighborhood games that many of us can recall so fondly are increasingly giving way to neighborhood gangs.

From this same magazine is a chart entitled "How Times Have Changed," which compares the top school disciplinary problems, as rated by the teachers, for the years 1940 and 1990. The chart reads from top to bottom with the greater infractions being at the top.

1940	1990
talking out of turn	drug abuse
chewing gum	alcohol abuse
making noise	pregnancy
running in the halls	suicide
cutting in line	rape
dress-code violations	robbery
littering	assault

In this same magazine is an article which addresses the growing fear our citizens have over the issue of crime. There is the senseless murder in Miami of the German mother—a tourist—who is beaten, robbed, then run over with a car in the presence of her six year old son. There are the six teens in Houston who are accused of the brutal rape then strangulation of two young girls who were taking a shortcut through a wooded area. By accident, they happened upon a scene where the boys were initiating two members into their gang. In New York, a teacher is shot in the back by four teenagers while in a park, just for his bicycle. As the writer of the article notes, "the outrageous has become ordinary. The obscene is commonplace."

Of course the changes are not just seen in our youth. Among adults, to give just one indication of the problem, workplace violence is on the rise. In 1991, in Texas alone, 117 murders occurred on the job. This makes homicide the leading cause of occupational fatalities in that state, at that time. It is as though we have become a people drunk on the wine of violence.

But it is not just the escalation of violent crime that is changing the face of our society. We are increasingly becoming a less civil people. Kindness and acts of what used to be called *common* courtesy are losing ground to rudeness and selfishness. Intolerance has become our national hobby. Customers rage at sales clerks when the item they wished to purchase is out of stock. Drivers, in a hurry to get to the next red light, cut off one another and ignore the traffic signals. (So serious a problem has this become that we now even have a name for it—*road rage.*)

In a crowded sandwich shop last week I saw a teenage employee hurt to tears by a rude customer in his early twenties. The customer could not believe that the young lady actually had to be told what type of sandwich he wanted. She had made the mistake of putting onions on his sandwich. "I said no onions!" he snapped. "I was just in here last week. I don't believe you can't remember how I like my sandwich. How stupid can you be!" The place was overflowing with customers. Crushed and humiliated, you could look into her face and tell that the young lady wanted to crawl off somewhere and die.

We are told by the psalmist that we were created just a little lower than the angels. What in the world has happened? What is wrong with us? It's simple, really. This is what a society looks like when the light is dying. Let me illustrate.

Where my family and I previously lived we had several tall crepe myrtle bushes (more like small trees really) which lined the front of our property. They were beautiful in bloom, alternately splashing deep whites and reds across the front of our lawn. One spring, I noticed that one of the white bushes lagged behind the others in growth. Crepe myrtles are incredibly fast growing but this one was having a bad run of it. Into the winter, with all of the foliage off, I decided to cut down the weakened bush and replace it.

As I swung my ax to the trunk of the small tree I was unprepared for what happened. The blade sliced completely through the eight-inch-thick trunk as though it were hot butter. Now, I'm strong, but not that strong. And my ax was sharp, but not that sharp. I nearly slashed into my own shin as the blade streaked through that trunk, lopping it off completely with just one blow.

I picked up the fallen crepe myrtle and examined the fresh cut. One look explained everything. Disease had struck the very heart of this bush and was killing it—from the inside out. How it had managed to survive the previous hot southern summer I do not know. At its heart, the bush was dead.

This simple story accurately illustrates the condition of our society. The pretense of life is there but our health is failing. Internally, the heart is not well. The light is dying.

Our Greatest Loss

I believe the most critical loss we have encountered as a society, the one thing more than any other that is moving us toward dystopia, is the loss of spiritual direction. Perhaps we have forgotten from whence we came. P. J. O'Rourke said, "America is where the wildest humans on the planet came to do anything they damn pleased." I love O'Rourke's writing, his humor, but he gets an *F* in history.

What an incredibly rich spiritual heritage we have as Americans. We are literally a nation founded by individuals who banded together around the common cause of spiritual liberty. Despite their numerous and well-documented flaws and screw-ups, these people were pursuing the freedom to develop the whole person, which they viewed as essentially spiritual. But we have lost this hunger as a people and have become, in Einstein's words, "a generation of improved means and confused goals."

Others have noted this about us. The former dissident of the former Soviet Union, Aleksandr Solzhenitsyn has eloquently and passionately stated this same case. In his address to the 327th graduating class of Harvard University, Solzhenitsyn warned that America's greatest danger lies in the fact that we are a nation which has become spiritually exhausted—a condition leading to ongoing social dystopia. Referring to this "calamity" (his word), Solzhenitsyn says:

> . . . a total emancipation occurred from the moral heritage of Christian centuries with their great reserves of mercy and sacrifice. . . . The West has finally achieved the rights of man, and even to excess, but man's sense of responsibility to God and society has grown dimmer and dimmer. In the past decades, the legalistic selfishness of the Western approach to the world has reached its peak and the world has found itself in a harsh spiritual crisis and a political impasse. All the celebrated technological achievements of progress,. . . do not redeem the twentieth century's moral poverty, which no one could have imagined even as late as the nineteenth century.[1]

Solzhenitsyn is exactly right. We are in the midst of a spiritual crisis. In the name of freedom and individuality, and under the guise of Enlightenment secularism, we have abandoned our spiritual heritage for a mess of pottage. This is our greatest loss. This is precisely why the light is dying in

---

[1] Aleksandr Solzhenitsyn, *A World Split Apart* (Harper & Row, Publishers, 1978), 51-52. This commencement address met with quite a volatile response. Enraged, not a few of those present walked out in the midst of Solzhenitsyn's address—a curious response for a university whose motto is "veritas" (truth).

our society and why we are coming more and more to sense that something is dead wrong with us. As I alluded to earlier, the thin veneer of civility which overcoats a barren and wayward soul is dissolving before our very eyes. Doug Minter is a young African-American who attended a local high school and is, at the time of this writing, a senior majoring in political science at the University of Tennessee. In a recent op-ed piece in our local newspaper he addresses the issues raised here better than a hundred politicians. His wisdom is greater than his years:

> As a young man now I look back on [the days of my childhood] and wonder what happened to the neighbor in the "hood." . . . The games of hide and seek have been replaced with real life games of hide or be killed and kick back or be beaten.
>
> Why is this happening? My mentors tell me that it is a simple lack of morality. We no longer have a sense of community in this country. Community is important as it is the traditional vehicle in which self-respect and the respect of others is born, nurtured, and protected. . . .
>
> White people cannot be the source for the condition of black people. Yet black people did not choose to live in a system which created the basic standards of life that we live under today. Let us not blame one another, for we have all acted as prodigal sons and it is time we return home. Let us all stand as individuals to produce solutions for the whole.[1]

Are we destined to continue on in this condition of social entropy? I do not for one minute believe this to be the case. Furthermore, I think that it is a good thing, in a paradoxical way, that we have come to where we are. Modernity has attempted to build society on the premise of a truncated self, leaving out the spiritual dimension of life.

---

[1] Doug Minter, "To Curb Violence our Communities Must Go Back to the Basics," *Knoxville News-Sentinel*, 6 February 1994.

And this can never succeed. Perhaps we had to get to this point before we would be willing to recognize the fact that along with the physical and social, we are also (and ultimately) spiritual beings. The sooner we return to this truth, the better.

If we continue down the road to dystopia it will be because this has been our choice. We are free to act. We are free to change. I believe that both individually and collectively it is our calling, our purpose to pursue our spiritual development. We need to be regenerated in spirit, just as Jung says. Spiritual and social attrition are not something which is inevitable. It does not have to be.

As I said in the introduction, this book is about recovering our dignity as human beings. It is a book of healing and hope, of redemption and restoration. It is about restoring our lives to the wholeness which is our birthright.

In order to do that we must understand how we got where we are. We now take up the subject of spiritual darkness for where there is a dying of the light there must be, of necessity, darkness.

It is, unfortunately, only too clear that if the individual is not truly regenerated in spirit, society cannot be either, for society is the sum total of individuals in need of redemption.[1]

—C. G. Jung

CHAPTER 2

Understanding Spiritual Darkness

It is impossible to understand our dilemma, let alone the solution, if we fail to understand that ultimately our predicament is a spiritual one. Men and women of insight have always understood this. Pierre Teilhard de Chardin pegs it exactly when he observes, "We are not human beings having a spiritual experience; we are spiritual beings having a human experience."

The Eden story in the book of Genesis reveals much to us about the subject of spiritual darkness. It takes us back to the basics. This is a fitting place to begin because, before we can ever hope to find a way out of our problem, we need to understand not only what is wrong but also how we got here.

We were created to walk in harmony with God and with one another. This is our high calling, as the archetypal couple in the book of Genesis illustrates. Chapter three gives the story. There, we are told that daily encounters with God were the common experience of Adam and Eve. They

---

[1] C. G. Jung, *The Undiscovered Self* (Mentor Books, 1958), 68.

walked with him and they shared both his companionship and his friendship as the three of them communed together there in that very special place. They thus experienced a transcendence in their lives which graced their earthly existence with a majesty and dignity. They were dual citizens, equally at home in both the physical and the spiritual worlds.

We should not quickly pass over the three attributes I have just used to qualify Adam and Eve's existence. I have described their experience as being _transcendent_ and _graced_ with _majesty_ and _dignity_. This is of great importance because these essential qualities are absent in so many lives today.

In my field self-esteem seminars have become a cottage industry. There would be absolutely no market for such a thing if transcendence, majesty, and dignity were restored to our daily lives.

Imagine someone saying, "I am experiencing life on a plane that far exceeds my five senses (_transcendence_) and I truly understand that I am the unique creation of a loving God—unique in all the world—(_majesty_) and that there is a noble purpose for my life (_dignity_). But, I don't know, I just feel so bad about myself." This would be an oxymoron of the highest order! The problem for so many people is that in their heart of hearts they do not believe their life to be crowned with majesty and dignity. They do not experience a transcendence in their day-to-day living. Consequently, there is a vacuum, an emptiness in their self-image.

A colleague of mine was working with a lady in her late twenties who was from one of the wealthiest families in town. She was a college graduate and a woman of some intelligence. Thanks to her parents' wealth she had traveled the world over seeing those sights most people only dream of. Her mother and father refused her nothing. Materially, what she failed to possess was pretty much due only to the fact that she had not asked for it.

This lady had been in therapy for a pervasive depression for several years. She had seen a number of therapists unsuccessfully prior to her work with my colleague and was on antidepressant medication. Within weeks he had assisted her to a major turnaround in her life. The therapeutic insight that allowed this client to turn the corner and pull out of her depression came in a session where my friend was firmly confrontational with her.

"Your problem," he told her, "is the triviality of your life." He went on: "You are an intelligent, gifted woman but you are wasting your existence. You have no career, you give no thought to your own personal growth, and you contribute nothing to the lives of others." (I am reminded of Jung's remark that the majority of people he had treated were not suffering from any appreciable mental illness but rather from the "meaninglessness and triviality" of their lives.) She was taken aback by his words. No one had ever talked to her like this. But to her credit, she hung in as he continued on. "All you do is sit around, living off your parents, indulging your empty life."

She had become tired enough of her life to apply his advice. In the subsequent weeks, together they devised a plan of action for her. Among other things, she started working as a photographer (something she had trained for) and she began meeting with a small group devoted to spiritual growth.

The changes which began to occur in her life were staggering—not the least of which was the fact that she soon pulled out of her depression. The key? She had begun the process of restoring meaning to her life, of putting value back into her existence.

Again, let us not pass by this idea lightly. To illustrate, I have worked with many substance abusers and can state categorically that I have never seen any addict who, prior to their addiction, held this high view of self. Moreover, the deterioration brought to someone's life by their chemical addiction only adds to the negative view of self which allowed for the abuse in the first place. It is thus a self-feeding downward spiral. Anyone familiar with the 12-step programs used in the treatment of substance abusers knows that the chief purpose of the steps is to place a sense of dignity into the minds and hearts of the abusers as to their intrinsic worth.

Think of the personal and social ills we see and experience that are directly related to a low and inadequate sense of self. This adolescent joins a gang because he experiences vicariously the strength he so painfully feels absent from his own life. This teen drops a tab of acid because she is out with a group she desperately wants to fit in with (to feel important, valuable) and they are all tripping.

This behavior is not limited to society's young. What strange behaviors we adults often engage in because of a desperate attempt to fortify an inadequate concept of self. The hundreds of millions of dollars which go annually to the cosmetic surgery industry alone can attest to this fact. (What a curious idea. "If I subject myself to enough physically altering surgical procedures, I think I will gain enough confidence to be myself.")

Slip Slidin' Away

Back to Adam and Eve. This couple experienced a life that was the intended birthright of us all. But something went awry. By an act of willful disobedience the bliss of this arrangement was shattered. By a solitary, deliberate choice (there can be no true freedom where there are no choices), the future of humankind was altered. After this fateful incident the subsequent scene in chapter three of Genesis is a pitiable one indeed.

While walking through the garden, the physical realm was once again pierced by God's presence. But all had changed. Rather than confidently approaching God as their desire and practice had been in the past, Adam and Eve dart for the bushes, hoping to hide from his presence. What a pitiful sight this is—a scene filled with fear and foolishness. Fear, now, of both the person and the presence of God. Foolishness, by the very nature of the act—attempting to hide from God as though he were a beat cop pursuing a criminal.

But this has been the instinctive nature of humanity ever since. First, to fear God and run from him. Second, to believe, in our foolishness, that we can hide ourselves from his attention and loving interest in our lives.

I often tell my clients that if we are not crazy and if we are not evil, there is a part within us that knows the truth. Adam and Eve illustrate this perfectly. Despite their efforts at concealment, they were very much aware that some fundamental change had taken place within them. How do we know this? Immediately after their disobedience, the narrative tells us, "And the eyes of them both were opened, and they knew that they were naked; and they sewed fig leaves together, and made themselves aprons."[1]

Speaking as a therapist, this is one of the most intriguing and insightful passages in all of literature, sacred or secular. It is pregnant with psychospiritual and psychosocial insight. I will say more about the psychosocial aspects of this verse later. First, I want to consider what this text tells us about the couple's attitude toward God after the fall. This is the psychospiritual focus.

Adam and Eve's nakedness was certainly literal. They had, to this point, lived without clothing. After the fall, they were so distressed, so embarrassed and ashamed, that they made coverings of fig leaves for themselves. Suddenly, and for the first time, the feel they have something to hide. How

---

[1] Gen. 3:7. Unless otherwise noted all scripture citations are from the *New International Version* (NIV), (International Bible Society, 1978).

strange, how uncomfortable this new emotion must have been for them. We have been hiding ever since.

To be sure, Adam and Eve felt ashamed of their physical nakedness, but there is a much deeper issue here. For the first time ever, Adam and Eve feel stripped down—naked in *spirit*. Imagine this. Imagine what it must have been like to experience, for the first time ever, a sense of inadequacy and imperfection. Feeling ashamed and unworthy, the last person they wish to see in this condition is God. They are painfully aware of being laid bare before him and yet at the same time they are afraid of this very thing. They are not just physically naked, they are spiritually naked as well.

Fear of God, not a reverence born of awe mind you, but abject fear, was never known by Adam and Eve previously. Such poisonous fear had never been in the human psyche, and was never intended for it. They are both unaccustomed to such fear and at the same time, unequipped to handle it. Improvising, they try to cover up lest they come face to face with God and his intimate knowledge of them. And they try to hide in the bushes, lest they have to give account.

Adam and Eve had lost their innocence.[1] They had lost it and they knew it. With innocence gone, what they really desire is to hide the inward effects of their deed. They cannot. They can only cover their bodies. In short, they compensate.

One wonders how much of the behavior we practice is an attempt to mask a naked heart. How often do we try to anesthetize ourselves with chemicals, materialism, even religion, in an attempt to sedate the inward voice? What defense mechanisms do we deploy in an attempt to hide the shame and conquer the fears? Despite our efforts, we end up looking

---

[1] Innocence is not to be confused with ignorance. The former is a state of freedom from cunning and guile, a condition of guiltlessness untouched by the ravages of evil. We can no more get back to innocence than we can un-fall off a roof or un-break an egg.

as pitiable as Adam and Eve in their newly-fashioned fig apparel. We may use different figs today but we look just as silly—and the results are exactly the same.

But this is the consequence of spiritual poverty. This is how we behave when the light has died . . . or the dimming has begun. We do not move toward God; in fear and shame we move away. We do not seek to nurture and nourish our spiritual development; we seek to conceal its very absence. In short, we abandon our greatest right and need—that of an ever-growing psychospiritual development.

Spiritual darkness is not only a matter of the inward person but of the outward as well. It is not only intensely personal, it is also imminently social. Like the personal, the social aspects of spiritual darkness are recorded for us in the Genesis narrative. One of the great popular misconceptions of our time is that spirituality is a strictly private affair and that, in point of fact, it is even vulgar to speak of such matters openly. This is most erroneous. There is nothing with more practical implications and direct influence on a society's health than the subject of spiritual pursuits. Again, this is why Jung says the regeneration of society is impossible apart from the spiritual redemption of the individuals which make up that society.

The social dynamics behind the events that took place that fateful day in Eden are staggering. In the attempt to cover their nakedness before God, Adam and Eve, in the process, covered up from one another. This is how it always works.

Just as the psychospiritual consequence of the fall was an attempt to hide from God, there is a psychosocial corollary. In their nakedness, Adam and Eve were ashamed before each other. They wanted to conceal, to cover up. Gone is the pristine nature of things as described before the fall, "And they were both naked, the man and his wife, and were not ashamed." I said earlier that the fig clothing was an attempt to hide from God, and this is true. But included in this ineffective endeavor is also the effort to conceal from one another. It should not escape our attention that what we have here is the archetype for the beginning of disingenuous, duplicitous relationships.

How deep and pervasive the change. Where there had previously been unity and harmony, the rules have changed. A different dynamic runs Eden now. It is now "every man for himself." We see this when God calls the couple to give account for their behavior. Before looking at this, a word about self-preservation.

Everyone is familiar to some degree with the idea of defense mechanisms. Basically, defense mechanisms are behaviors which are used to protect perceived inadequacies in the self and to defend against perceived attacks on the self. What we see in this passage is the birth of the ego and hence, the birth of defense mechanisms. Self-preservation rules. Do unto others as you wish, before they do it to you,—the so-called *iron rule*—is now the tenor of the times.

The Blame Game

When God confronts Adam and Eve we get a sad look at this new-formed human nature. While he wants to talk with each of them about their own behavior, their desire is to talk about someone else—*anyone* else other than themselves. In today's fashion, they paint themselves as *victims*.

God first asks Adam about his behavior. Adam promptly blames Eve for the deed done. Listen to him. "The *woman* you gave to me, *she* gave me of the tree, and I did eat." Adam says, in effect, "It's not my fault. I wouldn't have done such a dastardly thing on my own. It's that woman!" Adam, who had shared an intimacy with Eve never since known between a man and a woman now offers her up to God as the excuse, the party to blame for his behavior.

But it doesn't end there. Adam, in his desperation to find a scapegoat, blames God for the whole mess. Look again at his words, "The woman *whom you gave me* . . . ." In other words, "It's *your* fault God. If *you* hadn't given her to me this would never have happened." Adam was the first, although certainly not the last, to blame God for his troubles, even for his behavior.

Eve takes a different tack when God confronts her—one very popular today. Eve says, "The *serpent* beguiled me, and I ate." Eve is saying, "I could never be to blame for such a thing. The Serpent, it's his fault." It's almost comical. God excepted, the only credible party in the garden at this time is Satan! Adam blames both God and Eve for his behavior; Eve blames the serpent. Apparently, Satan blamed no one for his actions.

Same Tune, Different Time

In the thousands of years since the Eden story we have come no further. We are still hiding and hurling—hiding from God and from one another, and hurling our defenses and invectives.

Defense mechanisms always involve hostilities, perceived or real. This is a very important fact and supplies a partial answer to the spirit of violence and incivility pervading our society today. Think back to the garden. The air is thick with hostility. Adam and Eve are hostile before God and before one another. They are each perceiving the need to protect, to defend, their newly developed and damaged ego.

Scores of centuries removed from the Garden of Eden we are still playing the blame game. As I said, today everyone is a victim. It is the same old game with a different twist. "I am not responsible for my behavior," the line goes, "I am as I am and I do as I do because I have been victimized." Same game, new name.

At that time of this writing a court case in New York is generating a lot of media attention and national interest. The case centers around a murderous crime in which a lone gunman began firing into the passengers on the crowded subway in which he was riding. Several people were brutally slain and others wounded. Aside from the tragedy and waste of the incident the reason this trial is getting such attention is because of the strategy taken by the defense attorney. The defendant should not be held responsible for his action, the attorney contends, because as a member of a racial minority he is under the burden of accumulated racial rage and anger. Incredible.

Take another example. I recall a former client whose reputation had been damaged by a man (in a competing business) who had been verbally attacking him among their business associates and clientele. My client was most upset by the fact that the man had told a particularly severe lie about him. In one session, I was able to get both parties together for a meeting aimed at resolution and, if possible, reconciliation. Within the context of this session, my client confronted his accuser about the stories he had been spreading, and the untruthfulness of them. I will never forget the response the man gave nor the demeanor in which he gave it. Very calmly and without any apparent twinge of moral discomfort whatsoever he said, "I started those stories and I know they are untrue. However, I don't feel bad about it. I was under a lot of stress at the time." Forget, the damage done to my client's reputation. Forget the grief caused by the lies; the man bore no responsibility. Why? Because he was a victim of the stress he was under. The stress, not he, was to blame.

Victimization is the latest of our society's mantras. While out for a walk the other day I passed a pick-up truck parked by the roadside. Emblazoned across both the front windshield and the tailgate in stenciled, eight-inch letters were the words "Victim Of The Game." Apparently this guy is such a victim that he is victimized by all of society! Victimization reared its head in a prominent way in the middle of this century. Perhaps the greatest political monster of modern times, Adolph Hitler, rode to power in Germany on the back of the cry of victimization. In speech after speech he rallied support by declaring that Germany had been victimized by those who defeated her in World War I. She had been too severely restricted by the political settlements, too severely punished Hitler ranted. Germany was a victim.

Why are we like this? Assuming responsibility for one's self and one's behavior is foundational to psychological and spiritual health. What motivates us to abandon this ethic of personal responsibility and, instead, seek a scapegoat for our reckless behavior?

With victimization being all the rage today, the story of someone like Wally Amos is all the more refreshing. Wally Amos is a fifty-seven year old African-American who was raised in poverty and the segregation so prominent in that day. He was a high school dropout.

But Mr. Amos, armed with nothing but determination and his Aunt Della's chocolate chip cookie recipe, decided it was his responsibility to make something of himself. (Which is why he earned his GED while in the Air Force.) Through faith, grit, and hard work he turned his aunt's cookie recipe into an $80 million success—the Famous Amos Cookie Company.

Through some bad business decisions Wally Amos lost it all. He very nearly even lost his house! But Mr. Amos is undaunted. Despite the fact that a lost lawsuit disallows him to even use his own name with a food product, he has started another cookie company. Wally Amos is on the way up again. I have no doubt his success is due in no small part to his ethic of personal responsibility. Listen to him:

I never feel victimized. I take responsibility for what happened to me. That's what's important. You have to focus on what you *can* do. There are people who convince themselves that they can't do anything with their lives because of what's happened to them—and they're right. They can't. But the reason is that they've told themselves they can't. They've said 'I am a victim. Somebody did something to me that paralyzed me for life.' If you believe that, you'll never move forward.[1]

What causes us to abandon the ethic of personal responsibility? Why, like our archetypal parents Adam and Eve, do we try to hide ourselves from God and one another, prompting us to turn on each other in the process?

Why are we so capable of becoming preoccupied with little more than the preservation of an inadequate ego— and what provides the energy for this behavior which is both self and socially destructive? The shadow knows.

[1] Michael Ryan, "Why People Fail—and Why They Don't Have To," *Parade Magazine*, 22 May 1994, 4-6.

*Time watches from the shadow And
coughs when you would kiss.*[1]
—W. H. Auden

The Shadow Knows

In the intervening years since his death 34 years ago, Carl Gustav Jung has grown to be perhaps the most influential person in psychology today. To paraphrase Erica Goode,[2] more and more, in their quest to find meaning in life, many people are embracing the insights and teachings of Jung. To an ever-growing number of people conventional psychotherapy, which neglects and discounts the spiritual dynamic in life, is becoming less and less appealing. Many people are looking for something that speaks not only to their mind but their spirit as well. They are finding this *something* in the works of Jung.

Jung was born into a family with religious roots sunk deep and strong in its history. He had eight uncles who were ministers. His father was a Lutheran pastor. Jung himself was a man of intense spiritual devotion. In psychology, a field known historically for its animosity toward religion, many people consider Jung an oasis in an arid plain. For example, his genius and immeasurable contributions to psy-

---

[1] W. H. Auden, "As I Walked Out One Evening," in *Collected Poems* (Vintage Books, 1991), 134.

[2] Erica Goode, "Spiritual Questing," *U. S. News and World Report*, 7 December 1992, 64.

chology not withstanding, Freud is often deemed too petulant by the spiritually inclined. Jung, on the other hand, embraces the centrality of the spiritual in life.

The contribution Jung has made to the collective body of psychological theory is both immeasurable and invaluable. For example, speak of *introvert* and *extrovert* and knowingly or not, you are speaking Jungian. Jung was also the pioneer who introduced us to the notion of personality types.

Of the abundance of Jungian thought which is of such value to us today, the case could be made that his most critical idea for our times is that of the *shadow*. We will examine the shadow carefully in this chapter. However, it is important first to briefly explore a larger Jungian construct, which he termed *individuation*.

Jung considered individuation to be the ultimate goal of all psychological and spiritual growth. In defining individuation Jung says:

> Individuation means becoming a single, homogeneous being, and, in so far as 'individuality' embraces our innermost, last, and incomparable uniqueness, it also implies becoming one's own self. We could therefore translate individuation as 'coming to selfhood' or 'self-realization.'[1]

The individuated person is a united and unified self—a single, homogeneous being, as Jung says. Individuation means coming into our own; it means, in the fullest essence of the term, being ourselves. To individuate is to become all that we were created to be and all that is our right and responsibility to be. It is to move farther and farther into that majestic, transcendent experience of life that is our birthright.

---

[1] C. G. Jung, *The Collected Works of C. G. Jung*, 2d ed., vol. 7, *Two Essays on Analytical Psychology* (Princeton University Press, 1966; reprint, 1975), 13.

This is so very important. When we fail to pursue individuation, or we abandon that pursuit, we abandon our own uniqueness. In short, like Adam and Eve, we forsake our very personal and specific calling.

Jung believed there to be four stages in the process toward individuation. These stages occur not simultaneously but build one upon another.[1] For our purpose the stage of interest is stage 1, experience of the shadow.

The shadow side of personality is the part of each individual which he or she would like to disown. Great effort is made to distance oneself from the shadow—and to hide its contents from others. By instinct, we do not want to face the shadow and by that same nature, we want to conceal it from others. Listen to Jung's own explanation, "By shadow I mean the 'negative' side of the personality, the sum of all those unpleasant qualities we like to hide, . . ."[2] The shadow is the unconscious opposite of what the individual embraces and accepts into consciousness.

Because the shadow side of his personality is considered undesirable by the individual, a kind of duality is set up in the psyche. The acceptable and desirable portions of the personality are incorporated into the ego, while great effort is expended to repress and distance from the unwanted contents of the shadow. This behavior is as endemic to the human race as breathing.

We have all heard the expression, "She has a split personality." There is more truth to this than we realize. The shadow is indeed that part of ourselves that we attempt to split off from our personality. This explains why we are often caught behaving "out of character," as we say. In truth, this behavior is not out of character at all. It is behavior that

---

[1] Stages 2, 3, and 4 are encounter with the anima or animus, exploration of the archetypes, and the uniting of the self (self-realization).

[2] C. G. Jung, *The Collected Works of C. G. Jung*, 2d ed., vol. 7, *Two Essays on Analytical Psychology*, 66n.

is in keeping with a very real part of our nature. It just happens to be a part that we do not wish to own. Despite our best efforts to split it off from who we are, the shadow will not leave us. It remains attached just as does the shadow which accompanies our physical body. The shadow consists of components and aspects of our personality that are underdeveloped, immature, and inadequate. Because of their inadequacy, we expend great amounts of psychological energy in attempting to distance from these regressive aspects of our self. This is why I refer to the shadow as the unwanted baggage of the psyche. Our motive, although we are usually unaware of this, is to keep the shadow from rising to the consciousness of self, or the observation of others.

By stringing together the terms Jung used to describe the shadow, it is possible to get a better understanding of this integral component of our personality. Jung refers to the shadow as the "other side," the "dark brother," the "negative side of personality," and "the adversary."[1] He tells us the shadow is hidden, repressed, inferior, and guilt-laden.

John Sanford is an Episcopal priest and a Jungian analyst. Listen to this excellent description he gives us of the shadow:

> The shadow has been identified with primitiveness, violence, and cruelty. It constitutes the hidden powers of evil, lawlessness, and chaotic desires that, when released, bring about catastrophe. . . . It is the inferior part of our personality where we are . . . unadapted, irresponsible, psychopathic, and filled with infantile fantasies.[2]

The shadow has a kind of autonomy, operating independent from, and in opposition to, the conscious ego. It is the unconscious opposite of what we are willing to embrace about ourselves in our conscious mind.

---

[1] C. G. Jung, *The Collected Works of C. G. Jung*, 2d ed., vol. 9ii, *The Archetypes and the Collective Unconscious* (Princeton University Press, 1978), 286.

[2] John A. Sanford, *The Strange Trial of Mr. Hyde* (Harper & Row, 1987), 126.

Tying It All Together

Combining the Eden account with the idea of the shadow we can pull the picture into clearer focus. As a consequence of the fall we all (that is, all but the hopelessly narcissistic) realize that something is not quite right. We are incomplete somehow. When Adam and Eve came to consciousness of this fact they experienced a host of emotions and perceptions which were completely new to the human experience. Guilt, shame, fear, inadequacy—all new to the archetypal couple—had entered the picture. Imagine the feeling of suddenly being imperfect!

All of these perceived threats to the integrity of the self resulted in the birth of defense mechanisms, as we noted in chapter two. Recall my saying there that defense mechanisms are behaviors which are used to protect perceived inadequacies in the self and to defend against perceived attacks on the self.

The human psyche became overcrowded. I have never heard it described like this but, to me, this is the best explanation of the change which had taken place in Adam and Eve after the fall. There was suddenly a lot of stuff in there that the psyche was never intended to house. The Self lost its unity, its unification. (This explains precisely why the fourth and final stage of Jung's *individuation* is the uniting of the self.)

Some of their new-found feelings and perceptions were altogether valid. For example, there was a valid guilt called for. Adam and Eve had clearly defied the expressed command of God to them. Without the ability to experience valid guilt we would all be sociopaths. This is not the problem. The problem is that suddenly they were experiencing a lot of feelings which they were not equipped to process.

As I said, there is valid guilt—but there is also invalid guilt.[1] And this is true for all the other emotions and perceptions they were unexpectedly faced with. How to distinguish the valid from the invalid? When, for example, does valid shame turn to toxic shame? This was their problem. What is valid to be felt and perceived—and to what degree—and what is not? For example, should Adam and Eve have experienced valid guilt? Yes. Should they have felt that they were now despicable in the eyes of God and should run away from him? No.

Adam and Eve are thrown into a kind of psychic chaos. They are disoriented. Feeling threatened by all that they are suddenly experiencing, they turn to self-preservation. In a word— and this was a totally new phenomenon—they get *defensive*.

Every individual since that first couple has been born with the same problem—imperfection. And if that were not enough (At least Adam and Eve got to start on the problem as adults!) we are born to and parented by individuals who suffer that same affliction.

So what happens? A child comes into the world and she is innocent. As fully as she experiences her life—she lives it. But before long mom and dad start to register prohibitions. Sometimes the prohibitions are appropriate and are appropriately stated. Sometimes they are not. It all depends on where the parents are in their own development. At this point the child begins to experience exactly what Adam and Eve did, just on a smaller scale. Her psyche gets crowded and lacking the processing equipment, confused.

"I'm no good," is one way these parental prohibitions are processed. "I am ashamed of myself," is another. Parents who are loaded with all this same psychic baggage pass it on

---

[1] Invalid guilt is frequently called "false guilt" but to me this is a silly and inadequate term. It's like saying a soldier accidentally shot by one of his buddies was killed by a "false bullet." *False*, that is, invalid guilt *feels* no different than valid guilt and has the same affective consequence on the individual experiencing it.

to their kids. Imagine what happens in religious families if the parents are not mighty wise, perceptive, and in touch with their own shadow: "You had better be good because God won't like it if you . . ." It's into the shadow with all of this. This child goes off to school and learns from the teacher that "Nice children are polite and mannerly," for example. This child knows that sometimes she is not. So she feels bad about herself—into the shadow it goes.

Adolescence comes, and so does peer pressure. The teenager modifies her presenting self to find acceptance—distancing from those components of her personality which she deems (or worse, has been told) the group does not accept. She detaches from yet more of her true Self.

What happens when the adolescent becomes a young adult and falls in love? She marries a young man who has gone through the same process she has. By this time in life both of them have detached from more and more of their personality, repressing it into the shadow, and embracing only the acceptable self. The young couple has a child—and they start the whole process over again with him.

On and on it goes, self-perpetuating, self-defeating. At times it seems as though we are quite unable to distinguish between what is valid and what is not. Like Adam and Eve, we hide from ourselves, from one another, and from God. And in a never-ending attempt to protect our self, we erect our defenses and hurl our insults. Our psyche becomes more and more crowded as we split-off our self into acceptable and unacceptable (rejected) divisions. The negative side of the personality, the sum of all those unpleasant qualities we like to hide, get repressed into the shadow.

Robert Bly has a catchy way of presenting this idea. He refers to the shadow as "the long bag we drag behind us."[1] He says that we are born with a 360-degree personal-

---

[1] See Robert Bly, "The Long Bag We Drag Behind Us," in *Meeting the Shadow*, eds. Connie Zweig and Jeremiah Abrams, (Jeremy P. Tarcher, 1991), 6.

ity but as we encounter first our parents and then other significant individuals and peer groups in our life we continually slice of parts of our personality which meet with disapproval or resistance and put them in the long bag we drag behind us. Eventually, we end up with only a slice of personality and a bag full of shadow.

In the following section we will look first at specific case studies of the individual shadow and then the organizational shadow, as demonstrated in the church.

Part Two

ON THE DARK SIDE

The truth lies beneath the surface.
The surface lies.

CHAPTER 4

The Personal Shadow

We are all familiar with Robert Louis Stevenson's classic *Dr. Jekyll and Mr. Hyde*.[1] What you may not know is that *Jekyll and Hyde* is basically a study in the shadow. Dr. Jekyll was a Victorian gentleman, a handsome physician, a man of respect. He was distinguished in both life and work. He was, as we might say today, a model citizen. Although this was the Jekyll everyone knew, the good doctor was aware that there was another side to himself.

Dr. Jekyll became fascinated with the possibility of developing a way to let the two distinct and opposite personalities within him each have his own life. He began ceaseless experiments to this end. Finally, he developed a chemical powder that would permit him to change from the Dr. Jekyll whom everyone knew into his other self—Mr. Hyde. So successful was Dr. Jekyll's research that he was able to establish an independent identity for Mr. Hyde, even to the extent of providing him with his own residence in the Soho district of London.

Mr. Hyde was the very antithesis of Dr. Jekyll. He was a hideous creature, a "damnable man." Even his physical

---

[1] Interestingly, the basic story for Stevenson's book came to him one night in a dream.

structure differed from the doctor. He was raw power personified. He loved the cover of darkness as he skulked through the alleyways of London. There was a vileness to Hyde that both terrified and terrorized. He was dangerous.

For some time the experiment worked. Dr. Jekyll could live his responsible, respected life and then at will, by drinking the elixir, give rise to Mr. Hyde. This allowed the doctor to cater to his baser self without the risk of exposure. Nor was he troubled with guilt over the criminal exploits of Hyde for, he reasoned within himself, Hyde was truly another man—someone completely distinct from himself. This is the ultimate split personality.

Dr. Jekyll was the accepted self, the public persona. Hyde was the man of darkness, the man who wanted to work his works without ever being overtaken by the light. Thus, each man could be true to his own nature. It was a nifty arrangement . . . for a while.

Before long Dr. Jekyll discovered that he was losing control over Hyde. He began to be overtaken by the personality and appearance of his vile altar ego without use of the elixir. Hyde grew stronger as Jekyll grew weaker. Try as he might, the doctor could no longer control his self-generated rival. No longer content with attacking and killing others, Hyde craved to kill his creator so that he might live on, unimpeded by the good doctor.

In desperation, Dr. Jekyll turned to religion and piety. For two months he was back to his old self. Then Hyde returned. (As was inevitable. The superficial application of religion to a deep inner conflict can only bring a brief respite.) Worn down from the repeated effects of the elixir and by the tearing in his soul from the two natures, Dr. Jekyll dies.

Whether we like to admit it or not, we each carry within us our own Mr. Hyde. There is within us the shadow, the potential for dark living. This is exactly why Jung said we each harbor within ourselves a statistical criminal. We each possess within our own nature a destructive potential, the capacity for our own ruin. *Moreover, it is utterly impossible to grow spiritually without confronting this shadow.* The great laziness which most of us exhibit in this endeavor is the source of many evils, as we shall see.

The Case of Jill

Jill was a lady in her forties who was in the throes of a mid-life crisis. She and Mark had been married for some twenty-five years and were the parents of three children. Two years ago, Jill began illustrating the regressive behavior typical of a certain type of mid-life crisis as her behavior and attitude took a turn that was markedly adolescent in tone. She started compulsively buying many hundreds of dollars worth of clothing. Being in the lower middle class economically, this put a tremendous strain on the family's budget. All of the clothing purchased was much more in keeping with the styles of an adolescent than an adult. They were youthful, hip. Jill bought so much that her closets were overflowing. Often the clothes were not even removed from the bags but were simply stacked against the wall in her bedroom—back-to-back bags of clothing.

Jill began spending virtually every free moment at a local ski slope, often staying for as much as ten hours at a time with her newly acquired young friends. Because there was no one at home to keep them, the younger children had to tag along with their mother. (Due to overexposure to the cold, one of the children required medical attention.)

Jill was rarely at home in the daytime and soon began the practice of coming in very late at night, often after midnight. Mark would attempt to talk with her, voicing his concerns over her behavior. Jill insisted nothing was wrong with her and made it clear that she resented his questions.

A journalist by trade, Mark's work began to suffer as his worries increased.

Finally, Mark's suspicions were confirmed, his hunches validated. Jill was involved with another man. Mark had been told as much in an anonymous phone call. Now there was no doubt. He had found a letter written to the guy by Jill's own hand. Actually, the term "other man" barely fit the legal definition of the individual Jill was seeing. He was eighteen years old.

Searching about the house Mark found more letters along with some poetry and drawings that Jill had packaged together for her lover. The letters were adolescent in tone, as were the poems and art work. In fact, any casual reader who came across this material would swear it was from the hand of a fifteen-year-old. Mark was destroyed. The older child, who had found out what was going on from friends, was falling apart, being torn between feelings of abject shame and raging anger over what she perceived as betrayal of the family by her mother. To add to their humiliation, the daughter (a teenager) was told of her mother's affair by a mutual friend of the young man involved. Mark, who had all but lost the ability to do his journalistic work, now was given the near impossible task of attempting to console the older child. All of this while at the same time trying to keep everything hidden from the younger children and trying to maintain the normalcy of their small lives.

It was at this point that Mark and the adolescent came into therapy with me. Jill persistently refused to enter therapy. She would not hear of seeing me nor any other therapist, either alone or with her husband. Despite the havoc being reeked upon her spouse of twenty-five years, her children, and herself, she adamantly insisted that she had no problems. To compound things, she raged at Mark when he insisted she stop seeing her young lover. Furious, she railed at him, "Who do you think you are, trying to tell me who my friends should be?"

Not long after Mark and the oldest child entered therapy, Jill's amorous young friend ended the relationship. A letter Mark found indicated why. Ironically, Jill's lover found her too immature for his liking. Still adamantly refusing counseling because she denied having any problem, Jill soon replaced the lover who had jilted her with another colt of the same age.

Because she was unwilling to explore the contents of her shadow, Jill continued to reek great havoc on her family, not to mention adding to her own psychic turmoil. Unwilling to engage in the painful work of examining herself and her shadow, she continued on in her adamant denial. What a collection of psychic disturbances her shadow must have been, intensified by the fact that it was forced to become the harbinger of her ideations and behaviors surrounding her affairs.

All this suffering, all this sorrow to the family came about for one reason. Jill was a woman who refused to own and confront her shadow.

Rennie: A Brief Study

Rennie was one of the most intriguing clients I have ever had. He was the possessor of natural gifts that most only dream of. Rennie was also just about the angriest individual I have ever met. He had, as a result of his anger-induced behavior, seen the inside of a jail more than once. Rennie was in his mid-fifties when I first saw him. He had been married for many years but there was no relationship between him and his wife. Rennie treated her as nothing more than an object, a possession. The same was true of his treatment of his three children, all now grown and with children of their own.

According to his wife, home was miserable. It had been even worse when she and Rennie were younger and the children were at home. Rennie's anger routinely found in her body a target for his rage. Rennie ran the home like a fascist dictator. Nothing mattered but his will. There was no communication worthy of the name that ever took place in the home. His opinion was all that mattered. Indeed, according to his wife, it was the only one allowed. She described their home by saying, "It was as if the air was sucked out of the house because of him." There was no life when he was around.

Aside from his anger, Rennie's defining characteristic was rigidity. Despite the fact that his own life read like the biography of a gangland bully, Rennie was exacting and ruthless in his black and white judgment of others. Anyone who crossed his will or behaved in a way he disapproved of was summarily judged and discarded by him.

When I would point out to Rennie that by his own admission he had violated every standard he so strictly judged others by, he would agree briefly, but then proceed in his ranting, completely unfazed by this observation. It was his angry opinion that others should listen to what he had to say to them and then obey blindly and completely. I would once again attempt to show Rennie that his own checkered and misdirected life could not live up to the unbearable scrutiny he placed on others. This did not matter to Rennie. To him it was not even relevant to the discussion.

I saw Rennie only briefly and with no therapeutic success whatsoever. Other therapists who have attempted to work with Rennie had the same experience—brief involvement and no therapeutic change. If he lives to old age and does not radically change, I have no doubt that Rennie will spend his last days in lonely despair.

What makes Rennie tick? His shadow holds the answer. Rennie was as resistant to self-examination, which is all-important in confronting the shadow, as any individual I have ever seen. What a convoluted mess his shadow was. Because of his steadfast resistance to self-analysis, Rennie was a walking advertisement for projection.[1]

Furthermore, because he lives in abject unconsciousness Rennie constantly displaces onto others the judgment that rightly he should be using to evaluate himself. He judges others so severely because, living unconsciously, he has never judged himself. He cannot forgive others because he has never forgiven himself—because he has never judged himself (judgment always precedes forgiveness). Sadly, Rennie was completely oblivious to this entire process within himself.

God has made each of us to be the custodian of our own inner life. In that wonderfully rich New Testament word we are to be "stewards," stewards of our own soul. When we are not diligent in this charge we develop an increasingly pathological shadow. We then deteriorate, literally, from the inside out.

This observation is precisely what got Jesus in hot water with the religious leaders of his time. Attacking the duplicitous, shadowy nature of their lives he reserved his harshest words for the Pharisees:

> Woe to you, teachers of the law and Pharisees, you hypocrites! You are like whitewashed tombs, which look beautiful on the outside but on the inside are full of dead men's bones and everything unclean. In the same way, on the outside you appear to people as righteous but on the inside you are full of hypocrisy and wickedness.[2]

The fact that the Pharisees were aghast at the words of Jesus shows the utter unconsciousness which dominated their lives. They were offended, insulted that he would accuse them, the religious leaders, of being in such a pathetic state of soul.

---

[1] Projection is the unconscious, externalizing process by which one attributes to another the characteristics which are actually true of himself, but which he wishes to reject and disown.

[2] Mt. 23:27-28.

In decades gone by there was a radio serial which began each program with the familiar words "Who knows what evil lurks in the hearts of men? The Shadow knows!" Of course the radio program was referring to a different shadow, but how true these words are. The shadow does know! Adam and Eve would not have even dreamed themselves capable of such scapegoating behavior—but there it was. If someone had told the Jill of a year earlier that one day she would recklessly destroy her family she would have considered herself incapable of such things—but she did. Rennie contaminated not only himself but everyone around him with his hostile, unconscious living—but was oblivious to this and was convinced that the problem was everyone else. The Pharisees were certain that they were the spiritual giants of their time (and were quite proud of the fact!)—but Jesus appraised them as being walking tombs of spiritual decay.

Each of us possesses our own shadow. Housed in that shadow, or more correctly, comprising it, are all those attributes about self that we wish to disown, to deny. We try to ignore the shadow, to reject it. But these efforts are in vain. Whether we like the fact or not, our shadow is a part of who we are. Actually, the shadow is a more true representation of who we are for the simple fact that it lies closer to the Self (our true being) than does the conscious egocentric ego, which generates that persona we display to the public.

Later, we will discuss in detail just exactly what it is we are to do with our shadows. For the time being, the task is to recognize that we all possess this mysterious entity as an integral part of our being. For every Jekyll there is a Hyde. (Our first and greatest error on the road to psychospiritual growth would be to miss or to discount this fact.) It is true of your husband or your wife, your mother and father, your children. It is true of your boss and your co-workers, your neighbor and your doctor, your friend and your pastor. It is true of you, the reader. It is true of me.

It is, in fact, not only true of the individuals in your life, but of the organizations which you and I are a part of as well. This is the subject of chapter five.

He who fights with monsters might take
care lest he thereby become a monster.
And if you gaze for long into an abyss,
the abyss gazes also into you.[1]
—Friedrich Nietzsche

CHAPTER 5

The Organizational Shadow

The shadow exists wherever there is life. Each individual possesses a psychospiritual shadow just as his or her physical body casts a shadow.

However, not only are there individual shadows but also what might be termed collective shadows, shadows emerging from two or more people united together. There is a shadow side to the relationship between fiancees, and within families. Companies have shadows as do universities, committees, sports teams, and the local P.T.A. Congress has a shadow, as does the Pentagon and the White House. (A study of the shadow of the White House during the Johnson years—Vietnam, or the Nixon years—Watergate, would have been most interesting indeed.) Whole nations have shadows. Ultimately, there is the collective shadow of all humanity.

For our study of the organizational shadow I have chosen one of the oldest institutions in the world—the

---

[1] Friedrich Nietzsche, *Beyond Good and Evil* (Vintage Books, 1966), 89.

church.[1] Any organization could have been used for analysis but few offer so rich an insight into the collective shadow as does the church. Let me hasten to say, however, that any organization from the smallest (e.g., a couple) to the largest (e.g., a giant multi-national corporation) must be aware of its shadow and do shadow work, if it is to be healthy and thrive. It would be a great error for the reader to think that addressing the shadow is only applicable to organizations that are "spiritual" in nature or emphasis. Indeed, the wise business leader will not neglect to address the shadow aspects of her office or company.

(Prior to examining the church's shadow I would like to say a word about the appendix which I have entitled *Understanding the Church*. I feel this material is essential to the book but to include it here would obfuscate the purpose at hand. I would suggest reading the appendix before continuing with this chapter.)

Before beginning, I want to express four caveats. First, I hasten to my own defense to say that I do not make the following statements about the church either as an enemy, or as a provocateur. I am a member of the church, the body of Christ. I love the church. My entire early adulthood was spent in the pastorate. So the remarks I am about to make are not those of an outside observer. They are not the re-

---

[1] A word is in order here about the term "church." This word is used two ways in the New Testament to delineate two bodies of people: 1) to refer to a local assembly of individuals, e.g., the church in Corinth, and 2) as a reference to the vast horde of people—past, present, and future—who have or shall come to find in Jesus of Nazareth the ultimate meaning and significance of life. In the latter usage, the church is also referred to as the body of Christ. While the Body of Christ is visibly manifest to society through local assemblies, it should be noted that it is quite possible to be a member of *a church* without being a part of *the church*. Stated simply, one can be a member of a local church while, in reality, not being a part of the body of Christ. Unless otherwise specified by the context, the use of the term "church" in this book is a reference to the body of Christ as it is manifested to society through local assemblies (churches). At any given point in history, the two are contiguous.

marks of a theoretician, nor are they the remarks of an enemy. But honesty compels me to say that there are deeply disturbing trends observable in the church.

Second, please understand that I recognize my appraisal to be a most generalized assessment. I realize that there are local churches which are bathed in life and wholeness—churches which, in the fullest sense of meaning, are the pillar and foundation of truth, the salt and light of the world. My statement, and the thoughts which are to follow, regard what I believe to be the general flow, the spiritual condition of the American church when taken *as a whole*.

Third, we must understand that much of the true spirituality that exists in the world today is here because of the church. Without those unknown and unheralded saints who graciously give a cup of cold water in Jesus' name the world would be a much darker place. They demonstrate for us all what it means to be the light of the world.

Fourth, I realize that not everyone who is concerned with spiritual growth is in the church, nor is everyone in the church concerned with spiritual growth. (Indeed, probably most are not.) I remember talking to a man in town one evening when I was a college sophomore. We were on the subject of the spiritual life and in the course of that conversation I asked the gentleman if he were a Christian. He gave me a dagger-eyed stare and snapped, "What do you mean am I a Christian. I am an American aren't I!" To this man, Christianity was a matter of *citizenship*.

Allow me to recast this encounter slightly to illustrate what I believe many nominal Christians today are doing. I approach my imaginary Christian friend and say, "Tell me, are you involved in the quest? Are you pursuing your spiritual growth?" My (probably offended) friend retorts, "What do you mean am I pursuing my spiritual growth? I'm in church aren't I!"

To this person, spirituality is a matter of *membership*. This is a purely unscientific opinion, but I am not so sure that today there are not about as many people outside the church who are questing after spirituality as there are inside.

So, with these caveats out of the way, I proceed. Like our society at large, I believe the light of the church is dying. Why is there a dearth of spirituality in the church at a time when there is a resurgence of secular books on the subject and a renewed interest in the topic of spirituality among much of the general public?[1]

Largely, this is true because the church is not facing it's shadow. What do we expect to find in the shadow of the church? What barriers prevent the church from facing its shadow, and what are the consequences of this? These are the issues to which we now turn.

Resistance To Psychospiritual Growth

The initial aspect of the church's shadow to consider—resistance to psychospiritual growth—is indeed ironic. After all, this is the very thing the church is supposed to be about. There is really no need for the church to be on the earth apart from this pursuit of psychospiritual growth and development. The resistance which the church shows to this all-important pursuit manifests itself in two ways: 1) spiritual arrogance and 2) the fear of analysis.

The spiritual arrogance I am talking about is often aimed at psychology and reveals itself as the assumption that psychology has nothing of any benefit for Christians. There are vast treasures of understanding and insight into the human condition that go under-utilized by the church

---

[1] One of the counseling organizations I belong to has recently changed its name in deference to those who are in pursuit of spirituality but are not involved in an organized religion.

because of this arrogance. The argument runs something like this:

God has given us his word to show us how to live. Everything we need for our spiritual (and, by implication, psychological) well-being is in there. There is nothing which can or need be added. Psychology is, at best, suspicious and, at worst, of the Devil. The Bible is all we need.

If you are having emotional, behavioral, or relational problems, it is because you aren't praying enough, trusting God enough, reading his word enough, or walking in obedience to him.

I share with these detractors the belief that the Bible is our primary resource for psychospiritual growth. I really do. (If it were strictly an either/or proposition, I would keep the Apostle Paul and chunk Freud.) But to say that there are no other resources to aid our psychospiritual development is reaching and goes way too far. It is blatant pride.[1]

Further, I do not believe that Christians who hold this reductionistic view have thought it through. Otherwise, why would they read the devotional books, books on marriage and child-rearing, and the like, which are purchased each year by the millions?

Perhaps the following story will illustrate my point about this arrogance. David came to see me with an intense phobia that surfaced only when he was romantically involved. He had multiple marriages, at least one affair, and numerous girlfriends. David was a complex case. He had been severely abused, both

---

[1] A chance conversation I had with a stranger (who, it turned out, was in Christian ministry) at a local golf course illustrates my point. We both happened to be waiting to pick up our sons from a round of golf and we struck up a casual conversation. He asked about my occupation and when I told him I am a psychotherapist he looked at me a moment, mumbled "hmmm," and then spoke. These were his words: "Don't you have a problem with that? Those people don't believe in truth." I'm not sure which impressed (depressed?) me more, the arrogance of his words, or the ignorance. I have never met a therapist or counselor of any stripe that does not believe there is such a thing in life as truth, though definitions may vary.

physically and emotionally as a child. Also, childhood had been without any positive bonding with an adult who could have helped him weather that critical period of his life. He was now middle-aged.

One day, not long into therapy, David came for his regular session. He was angry and obviously confused. He "sat in on me," as we say in the South, as soon as he was seated:

> I think this therapy is a waste of time and money. If you could do any good you should have cured me by now. All I need is God. . . .If I just had more faith, my problems would instantly disappear because God would heal me. . . .I will never get better as long as I come to you because this proves that I am not trusting God.

I listened quietly, trying to sort David's peculiar new attitude out in my mind. I had known from the outset that he was from an authoritarian, conservative church background which looked upon psychology with a tendentious eye. However, David did not share this view. I was therefore surprised when he came out with this uncharacteristic ranting.

After allowing David to vent his angry thoughts, I asked him where this stuff had come from. "This doesn't sound at all like you," I said. At this, David's expression changed. He no longer looked angry, just confused—and very, very sad.

In words lacking in both energy and air David said, "My family has been after me." He continued:

> They said I had been coming to you for several weeks now and you still have not cured me. They are telling me that I am showing God that I don't have faith by coming to you. That's why he won't heal me, they say. They tell me that my sister "went forward" in church last Sunday and rededicated her life to the Lord and that I should see

the change in her.[27] They say I need to quit seeing you, trust God, and let him do for me what he did for my sister.

This sort of pressure continued from the family until David quit therapy two weeks later.

For years I, and many others, have written and lectured on the imperative psychology faces of recognizing the important role of spirituality in the human psyche, and in the study of human behavior. In one form or another we have all stated that a psychology which ignores human spirituality cannot possibly be a complete psychology. I have stated that the arrogance demonstrated toward psychotherapy by the church is ironic. This is what I mean. Much of the church is as resistant to psychology as the majority of the clinical community is to religion and spirituality. Often, I think that if the psychological community comes to realize the centrality of spirituality in the human psyche the job is still only half done. We must then turn our efforts to the task of persuading the church of the value of psychology.

Recall my saying that I believe the church's resistance to spiritual growth reveals itself in two ways. We have just observed the first, which I have labeled spiritual arrogance. Let us now turn to the second cause of resistance namely, the fear of analysis.

Therapy requires courage. There are a lot of skeletons in our closet, to use the familiar adage. (Or perhaps we are more like Burt Reynolds characterized himself once on TV

---

[1] Katie, David's sister, was also middle-aged but slightly younger than he. Her life was a mess. Every few months Katie would go to church, "go forward and rededicate her life," and actually change—for a few weeks. After a short period, she would revert to type. It was one of Katie's short-lived ostensible renewals that their family was euphorically using as ammunition against David. The fact that Katie's repeated "rededications" had caused no lasting change in her behavior, coupled with the fact that she continued to deteriorate psychospiritually were selectively ignored by the family.

saying, "I don't have skeletons in my closet, I have whole bodies!") There is an innate fear of being seen, of being found out. Remember Adam and Eve? Embarrassing behaviors, past failures, shattered dreams, horrible memories, heart-breaking losses—and perhaps most of all, the customized, made-to-fit narcissism we each posses by nature—make us afraid to enter therapy. However, deep down, unless we are sociopathic, we know there is work to be done. There is just a natural tendency to fake it rather than fix it.

There is a particular incongruity in the fact that the church, which claims a mandate from God to pursue spiritual growth, would fear analysis so extensively. "Examine yourselves . . . test yourselves," the Apostle Paul says.[1] What are we afraid of?

There is so much repression observable in the church—and so much suppression, of the unhealthy variety. Let me hasten to add that there is perhaps no more than in society at large, perhaps not even as much. But remember, society does not claim to be "the pillar and foundation of truth," the "salt of the earth," or "the light of the world," (see appendix). This burden, this responsibility—this claim—applies only to the church. Psychospiritual growth is *at the very heart of what the church is supposed to be all about.*

One characteristically sees Christians compensate for this fear of analysis by using what I have come to call verse-stamping. Verse-stamping is really a kind of ecclesiastical defense mechanism which is employed to circumvent a deeper analysis. It amounts to a superficial application of scriptural truth.

A friend and I remember with fondness and a good laugh an incident from a few years past. Gordon had been acting a little unusual of late, as though he were carrying a great weight in his mind. One night he called me and asked if we could get

---

[1] 2 Cor. 13:5.

together for a bit and talk. I happened to be free that evening so I went right over. I picked Gordon up and we drove around for hours talking.

It turned out that my friend had committed an act a few nights previous which had caused him much grief and guilt. Gordon said, "I have prayed about this over and over and for a while God gives me peace but later the guilt and shame return." As we talked my friend would ask questions and then before I could reply, would answer them himself with a series of biblical quotations, that is, verse-stampings. After about thirty minutes of this I reached over and put my arm around Gordon's neck and told him laughingly that if he quoted one more verse to me I was going to tape his mouth shut. Was I being disrespectful of scripture or undermining the importance of biblical insight? Not at all.

Gordon was not utilizing the wisdom of scripture to confront his behavior and find forgiveness, healing, and understanding. Rather, he was using it as band-aids, or as a kind of mental bumper sticker. Gordon is a good man with a good heart. He is imminently teachable and passionately devoted to his own psychospiritual development. He understood precisely my meaning. With characteristic integrity Gordon responded. "I know what you're saying. I guess it is just easier and less frightening to quote a verse than it is to look at myself and this mess."

Verse-stamping is a twisted and superficial use of scripture. In the song *Take Me Back* Van Morrison sings prayerfully and from a longing heart for an understanding of religion. You never hear that in the church. Everybody just acts like "We Christians *know*." (And perhaps no one is more afflicted with this malady, more tempted toward it than pastors.) As I have said, the employment of verse-stamping belies a fear of analysis. Listen to these words from the New Testament book of Hebrews. "For the word of God is living and active. Sharper than any double-edged sword, it penetrates even to dividing soul and spirit, joints and marrow; it judges the thoughts and attitudes of the heart."[1] Truth penetrates to the very core of our being—to soul and spirit, to the thoughts and attitudes deep within us. Nothing superficial here.

As I said previously, resistance to psychospiritual development is perhaps a surprising thing to find in the shadow of the church. It is there nonetheless. As we have just seen, this resistance manifests itself in spiritual arrogance and in the fear of analysis.

Sexuality

Human sexuality is a component which occupies a huge space in the church's shadow. Despite twenty centuries of trying (or perhaps not trying), the church has never come to grips with this subject. This is precisely why sexual neuroses abound in the church. One comical but telling illustration of this point is in the treatment the Old Testament book Song of Solomon has received through the centuries.

The Song of Solomon is the romantic tale of the sexual attraction and sexual life between Solomon and the wife he loves, the Shulamite maiden. It is a beautiful recounting of their cathectic experience and their relationship together. In graphic, explicit detail Solomon describes their sexual attraction to one another as well as their love-making. (Would it surprise you to know that Solomon and his love practiced French kissing long before there were any French to kiss! See 4:11 and 5:13) Oral/genital caressing, fondling, the deepest experiences of sexual foreplay and love-making. It's all there.[2] What a primer this book is on love—and love-making between husband and wife.

---

[1] Heb. 4:12.

[2] See, for example: 2:3, 4:16, 5:1-16, 6:2-3, and 7:1-13.

Through the centuries, however, the church divines have managed to put such a fanciful allegorical twist on this book that it would cause even Origen[1] to blush! The church has been told over the ages that the book could not possibly be about *that*. So, the idea was popularized that the Song of Solomon is really an allegory about Christ and the church. I cannot verify it but my suspicion is that this hermeneutic was first spun by someone in a fit of distemper.

To believe this interpretation of Song of Solomon, one has to accept that in the midst of the Old Testament chronicling of God's dealings with Israel, he paused to insert a book about Christ and the church—and a most sensual book at that. This would have made absolutely no sense to the Jewish readers of that time whatsoever.

This interpretation of the Song of Solomon surely has as its origin the sexual neurosis of the church, a neurosis which has given birth to all sorts of bizarre practices. Let me illustrate.

In 1985 I was on a teaching tour in eastern Europe. A German cleric recounted to me the story of a common practice engaged in by a denomination there in bygone generations. When a man and woman married, the elders of the church would accompany the newlyweds to their bed chamber on their wedding night. The bride and groom were given simple linen gowns to put on, each of which had a hole strategically cut in the front midsection. As the time came for the couple to consummate their marriage the elders would approach the bed and stand close around it. The groom then assumed the "missionary position" (telling name for it, eh?) atop the bride. At this point, he was to insert his penis through the hole in his gown—how he managed an erection I will never know—through the hole in the bride's

---

[1] Origen was a theologian of the third century known for his allegorical interpretation of scripture.

gown, and into her vagina. The elders were there to ensure that the couple did this properly without engaging in any "carnal" positions or "getting into the flesh" by enjoying themselves. My guess is that the only people there enjoying themselves were the elders! Talk about shadow![1]

Thankfully, today there is an emergence of literature celebrating the Song of Solomon for what it is, God's sanction and celebration of human sexuality. The former view is deeply rooted however, and dies slowly.

By repressing sexuality into the shadow, all sorts of sexual outbursts spring forth in the church. This is such a common fact that I would indeed be surprised if there is a single reader who has not heard of some sort of sexual fall in a church they attend or are familiar with. Remember this maximum: the shadow will not be denied. Let me give one brief illustration of this.

I am familiar with a church in which the senior pastor was found to have been amorously involved with a married lady in the church. The Board of Elders brought this matter before the church for a vote to dismiss the pastor. (This church adhered to a congregational form of polity.) As it turned out, this pastor was sexually involved with several of the ladies in the church. When the matter came up for vote there was a turn of events that, to say the least, shocked the Board. Rather than dismissing the pastor, the congregation voted to dismiss the Board of Elders and keep the minister. It seems the pastor was extremely popular with the women of the church and they rallied together to save his job! An

---

[1] This brings to mind another story of sexual neurosis in the church. After her husband, Prince Albert, died, Queen Victoria was in constant and pervasive grief. Attempting to console her, a lady-in-waiting spoke of the great people from the Bible the Queen would meet in heaven. When she mentioned King David, Victoria snapped, "No! No! I will *not* meet David!" (because of his sexual transgression). David was spiritual enough to write the book of Psalms but apparently not spiritual enough to share heaven with Queen Victoria!

extreme illustration of the point perhaps, but an accurate and factual one nonetheless.

Divorce

Another component of the church's shadow is the subject of divorce. The church has always been a bastion in support of the sanctity of family. The bedrock of this is a strong affirmation of the institution of marriage. This is good, especially today when it seems so many people marry or divorce with little more thought than they give to what condiments to order on their cheeseburger. But there is a shadowy nature to the way in which the church treats those who have suffered through the wrenching ordeal of divorce.

In the church, divorce has taken on the stigma that leprosy held in ancient times—and the divorcee has become the leper. The gambit of alienation runs the scale from social estrangement within the church to disallowing membership entirely (ostracizing). It is not uncommon to see churches where divorced men and women are allowed to mow and tend the grounds, perform custodial chores, work the nursery during service, or prepare food for church socials, but they are not allowed to hold positions of leadership such as sit on boards or teach classes. To be sure, there is a lot of verse-stamping as to why this is so, depending on this or that group's particular interpretative bias, but there is no sound authority for doing this. The motivation has much more to do with a fearful shadow than with hermeneutics. How many people already struggling with the devastation and psychological baggage concomitant with divorce have I seen brought even lower by the comments, treatment, and nonverbal messages received from both pulpit and pew.

Steve fleshes out this matter for us. I first came to know Steve when I was a pastor. He was doing some repair work on my car at the time. He was a former military man with a mind as sharp as a razor and the self-discipline of a drill sergeant. After this brief contact I heard nothing more from Steve—nothing more until three months later. One evening Steve called me at home and asked if he could schedule a session with me. I knew something serious was up. He was not the kind of man to share his troubles. Steve had his demons. He had come from a particularly tough childhood that made close relations agonizingly difficult for him. He was an angry man and though never physically abusive to anyone, he seemed to be one step from blowing. He was wired tight. I was not ready for the broken man who came into my office that night.

Steve's wife had recently divorced him and was granted custody of their teenage son and daughter (twins). The expense of the divorce along with the alimony/child support payments had busted Steve financially. He had moved from his comfortable home into a modest apartment and was trying hard to make ends meet. As he told the story, Steve's usual character and candor were present. He was not bitter at his wife, even though she refused to seek intervention for their marriage. In her words she had simply "had it." Moreover, Steve stated very candidly that the cause of the divorce was overwhelmingly his personality and behavioral style. He owned this as an accurate statement of the facts.

As devastated as he was by all of this, Steve's primary purpose for calling me was something else. As he unfolded his story further, Steve began to cry. He was a broken man.

This is what happened. Steve had admitted to his church that he was divorcing and that he was mostly to blame. From that moment on, although his continued attendance was allowed, Steve was an outcast at church. People would not sit with him, would not even talk with him in anything but the most superficial way. With tears in his eyes Steve said to me, "Mike, I could have murdered my wife and they would have forgiven me. But they won't forgive me for the divorce, even though I didn't want it." He went on to say, "It was hard enough losing my wife and children. But with the added rejection of my church, I have no one. I can't take this."

What is behind this hurtful posture toward divorced people? The ready answer is that divorce is sin. Okay, fine. But this in no way excuses the cruel treatment of divorced people by the church. Let me suggest another, more shadowy reason. Psychologically, I believe much of the posturing that occurs in the church regarding divorce and divorced persons is a reaction-formation emanating from the church's shadow.

Many people in the church experience a marriage that is, to say the least, less than satisfying. I believe that divorced people often stir the shadow of a lot of churchgoers by alerting them to the tenuous ground their own marriage is on—and the unsatisfying nature of that marriage. To be candid, I know for a fact that many of these people secretly long for a divorce themselves (because they have told me so). I am, of course, not in the least suggesting that they should get a divorce. I am, however, suggesting that they be aware and be honest about where they are in their own marriage, and then do the hard work necessary for improving their marriage. And beyond that, I am suggesting that they not project their own shadow issues onto the broken and wounded people who have experienced the pain of a divorce.

Emotional Constriction

Another significant aspect of the church's shadow relates to emotional constriction. Of the full scope of human emotion, the church seems willing to accept into consciousness only a narrow band of feelings—feelings I refer to as the ecclesiastical emotions. Such feelings as guilt, sinfulness, conviction, joy, blessedness, humility, shamefulness are commonplace in the church. But locked away in the collective shadow are the prohibited emotions of greed, lust, pleasure, anger, ecstasy, and so on. I am not arguing the relative value of such emotions. I am merely saying that they exist. They exist and they are common experiences for Christians, just as they are for all other people. Anyone who refuses to admit to this is not being holy, he is being something less than fully human.

Confusing emotions with behavior, Christians have selectively divided emotions into categories of acceptable and unacceptable. The unacceptable feelings do not evaporate, however. Rather, they become part of the shadow, where they do their work in darkness. When this occurs, the repressed and inappropriately suppressed emotions behave like the smoke in a chimney with a closed damper. Start a fire in a closed chimney and the smoke seeps first into the room and after that, through and out whatever cracks it can find around the doors and windows. That is what these unwanted emotions do. They seep through the cracks in the personality in a thousand different ways.

The idea behind this division of the emotional life into acceptable and unacceptable components seems to be that the Christian should not experience many of the feelings common to all humans. Let me illustrate.

A client and I were discussing a recent movie on the life of the famous Christian writer and thinker, C. S. Lewis. I commented that I thought the movie was excellent and that I had, in fact, seen it a couple of times. My client responded, "I liked the movie, all but the ending. I didn't like the way Hollywood made it look like C. S. Lewis got mad at God because his wife got cancer and died." I said, "But he did get angry. And for a while he stayed angry. Lewis's own writings makes this clear." (Interestingly, both her verbal and nonverbal cues demonstrated that she was angry at "Hollywood" for portraying Lewis as angry! Of course, she was unaware of her anger.)

As the helpful research of Elizabeth Kubler-Ross shows, anger is a clearly defined and recognizable step in the grieving process.[1] It was only natural that Lewis go through an anger stage in his grieving. Not to do so would not have made him more spiritual, it would have made him less than human.

But this lady's attitude is so typical of how the church handles the "unacceptable" emotions. The thinking, in this particular example, runs like this: "Anger is wrong. Anger at God is *certainly* wrong. Therefore, Christians shouldn't get angry and spiritual Christians (e.g. C. S. Lewis) simply don't do so." Of course, this does not evaporate the anger at all. Rather, the individual merely dissociates from it. The anger is repressed and becomes part of the shadow. Some of the angriest people I have ever met in my life are Christians. Henry Drummond, the nineteenth-century scientist and minister in the Free Church of Scotland, echoes this idea saying "It is highly moral people, *unaware of their other side*, who develop particularly hellish moods." (What insight!) And they will be in church this Sunday wearing a gospel smile but with a shadow that resembles a hopelessly cluttered garage. If they will admit to anything at all they will say they are "concerned" or "burdened"—anything but mad.

A comical example of the emotion of anger is illustrated by a former client, Valerie. Valerie was seeing me for a mild depression that had crept into her life and become quite pervasive. Barring biochemical origins, when someone seeks treatment for depression a good rule of thumb is to look for the anger. It's almost always there somewhere.

Valerie's focus seemed to be on the husband of her recently married only child. As she discussed her son-in-law, Valerie's nonverbal communication contradicted her words. It seems that Jim, the son-in-law, had quite a checkered past and

---

[1] In order, the steps are shock/denial, anger, bargaining, depression, acceptance.

Valerie was most dubious of him. She was convinced that Jim had married her daughter only for the inheritance (the family was extremely wealthy).

I asked Valerie to share her heartfelt attitude toward Jim because I suspected that we would find the root of her depression there. "Oh, I love him," Valerie remarked. "We sit together in church and see each other nearly every day. Jim has even begun helping me with my Sunday School class." Valerie's answer sounded polite enough but my clinical sense was just not buying it. I shared with her how that often we Christians—believing we should not feel certain ways—will try to overcome those feelings by ignoring them. I explained that we were not attempting to place a positive or negative value on her feelings, that we were merely trying to recognize them and that this would help us greatly in knowing what we were dealing with. I assured Valerie that I understood that her motivation was noble, that she felt it would be wrong before God to hold certain attitudes and that she was giving every effort not to have them. I told her that the fact is, right or wrong, she feels what she feels and that is where we had to start.

Valerie was silent for a minute—a long minute—and then she slid forward in her chair. Gripping the chair arms she looked side-to-side as if to reassure herself that we were alone and leaned toward me. She looked me square in the eyes and then with taught jaw she said through gritted teeth: "Do you really want to know how I feel about Jim?" Before I could answer she said, "I'd like to punch his lights out!" Then for a brief couple of minutes all sorts of suppressed material poured out. She spoke of how Jim had married her daughter for the money, was not worthy of her, and on and on.

Not three minutes into this tirade Valerie began to laugh. "Man, that felt good," she said. The anger was out. That quickly the depression began to lift. Because she had owned her feelings we were now able to develop a plan of action. Valerie had a long heart-to-heart with Jim who, as it turns out, was struggling with some rather powerful feelings he was having toward Valerie. Although the two never became the most intimate of friends (and likely never will), the relationship between Valerie and her son-in-law began to improve and was now at least on amiable and honest grounds.

We must recognize that the presence of certain "unacceptable" emotions is not the same as sanctioning these feelings. It is simply to say they exist and are being experienced—period. Doing this is often the turning point for successful therapeutic intervention and is absolutely essential for spiritual growth.

But this fact of emotional suppression and denial is not true just for what we might call the negative emotions alone. Susan, my wife, and I were attending a small dinner party at the home of one of the couples we pastored. Two other couples from the church were there along with other members of the host's extended family. After dinner we were sitting around sharing anecdotes and I noticed that one of the relatives of our host would peer over at me each time someone got to the punch line or funny conclusion of their story. After about four episodes of this I asked the lady, Sally, why she was doing this. Her reply was quite funny. Sally said she had never seen this sort of lightheartedness around a pastor and she was wanting to see if I laughed at the stories! She thought it was terrific that church members would be jocular around their pastor and that the pastor would not only enjoy this but also join in. Somewhere along life's way she had picked up the idea that Christians and certainly pastors are dour people.

Of Bias and Bigotry

There is one final aspect of the church's shadow which is important to address and that is the matter of racial, socioeconomic, and gender bias. There is much to be said about each of these issues separately. In fact, whole books could easily be written on each of them. In lumping these concerns together I do not imply that they are of lesser importance. They are, however, similar, and therefore can be addressed conjointly.

St. Paul says "In Christ's family there can be no division into Jew and non-Jew, slave and free, male and female. Among us you are all equal. That is, we are all in a common relationship with Jesus Christ."[1] If this be true then the church has much to answer for. Let us look briefly at Paul's assertion.

Paul claims that there is racial equality in Christ. Actually, this is not exactly accurate. What he really is saying is that in Christ there is racial irrelevance. It just doesn't matter. It's unimportant. But one would never know that by the church. Although, thankfully, there is progress in this area, the fact remains that churches are divided along racial lines. There are black churches and there are white churches. There are Korean churches and there are Latino churches. While I suppose it is possible that this is just a matter of preference, I tend to believe the answer is a lot more shadowy. I am afraid that it indicates that we really do not grasp the meaning of Paul's words. Some would say it is a matter of separate but equal. I do not think this holds up. If this were true, how could it be said over and over in scripture that we are all "one body?"

Paul goes on to say that in Christ we are neither slave nor free. Slavery was standard fare in the Roman world of New Testament times. In all probability the majority of early Christians were slaves. Thankfully, we do not have to confront the matter of slavery in the church today. What we do

---

[1] Gal. 3:28. This translation is from Eugene H. Peterson, *The Message: The New Testament in Contemporary English* (NavPress, 1993). All future citings from this translation will be annotated *THE MESSAGE*.

face, however, is an issue that went hand-in-hand with slavery and that is the matter of socioeconomic status.

Just as most churches are divided along racial lines, so to are they divided socioeconomically. We have poor churches, middle class churches, and wealthy churches but rare indeed is the church that has a blend of all three. All sorts of comical games arise from this. The wealthy are convinced the poor show up only to "get something." The poor are certain the wealthy attend church "just to be seen" and that they, by the very fact of their wealth, cannot possibly be spiritual. The middle class churches just seem to aspire to the one while trying hard to avoid the other.

Now of course there are churches where this is not the case; but there is a real temptation toward these tendencies. This is a problem as old as the church itself. James writes:

> If a man enters your church wearing an expensive suit, and a street person wearing rags comes in right after him, and you say to the man in the suit, "Sit here, sir; this is the best seat in the house!" and either ignore the street person or say, "Better sit here in the back row," haven't you segregated God's children and proved that you are judges who can't be trusted?[1]

Socioeconomic divisiveness is stern stuff in God's eyes. Earlier in his epistle, James gives a sensible, balancing truth about the matter of socioeconomic status. He writes, "The brother in humble circumstances ought to take pride in his high position. But the one who is rich should take pride in his low position, because he will pass away like a wild flower" (1:9-10). The point is not that wealth is right and penury is wrong or that the opposite is true. The point is that both

---

[1] James 2:2-4, *THE MESSAGE*.

exist, that we need each other, and that we have much to learn from one another.[1]

In the last of his three couplets in the Galatians passage Paul says that, just as racial and socioeconomic distinctions are irrelevant, so too are gender differences. There can be no division into male and female, Paul writes. The male domination that permeates the church creates two immediate problems worth noting.

First, the church is robbed of the opportunity to see the more "feminine" aspects of God's personality lived out in its midst. God has emotion, is creative, imaginative, passionate, nurturing, tender. He is compassionate, gentle, protective. I think the church is imbalanced toward a left-brained logic oriented approach which is characteristically male and which diminishes these (typically considered) feminine aspects of God's nature. This is the direct result of failing to utilize the gifted women Christ has given to the church over the years.

I have a theory as to why the Apostle Paul is generally the most beloved of all the Apostles and why we are drawn to him. In Paul's character we see a marvelously whole individual. He was tough—and yet he was tender. He was strong and logical and could hold his own in any debate or discussion. And yet he was gentle, long-suffering, gracious, and compassionate. He could confront Peter publically and to his face when he was behaving duplicitously. Listen to Paul: "Later, when Peter came to Antioch, I had a face-to-face confrontation with him because he was clearly out of line."[2] And yet he could tenderly nurture the weakest of his fellow believers. He writes to the Thessalonians,

---

[1] I might mention the fact that the Bible does not factor the middle class into its socioeconomic discussions for the simple fact that there was no such thing. The middle class is a modern development.

[2] Gal. 2:11, *THE MESSAGE.*

"We were never patronizing, never condescending, but we cared for you the way a mother cares for her children. We loved you dearly. Not content to just pass on the Message, we wanted to give you our hearts. And we did."[1]

The second immediate problem which has arisen from the male domination of the church is linked to the first discussed above. Because women have historically been denied the right to rise to positions of leadership in the church, they have often resorted to unfortunate methods of obtaining power. To be candid, this male dominance has generated as a shadowy backlash a constituency of women in the church who are quite manipulative. Now, let me say that I do not believe that the majority of women in the church are manipulative any more than I believe that the majority of men are chauvinist pigs. But the fact is, anyone who has spent much time at all as either a member or a student of the church realizes that very often the most powerful block in any given church is that certain woman or unofficial group of women. It is rare to see this woman (or contingency of women) *overtly* manifest this thirst for power, but manifest it she does.

I recall from a few years back, a congregation I was familiar with. The church was strongly committed to the male leadership position. Women were allowed to teach children and other women but that was it. Further, women were not permitted to serve in any administrative or congregational capacities whatsoever. Publically, the pastor was totally dogmatic about the fact that this is the only arrangement God approves of. Hardly a sermon passed but what he somehow managed to work this theme into his message. Nevertheless, church insiders saw quite a different picture.

---

[1] 1 Thes. 2:7-8, *THE MESSAGE.*

The fact of the matter was that this pastor's wife was actually the one in control of the church from behind the scenes. A mere word from her was enough to get Sunday School teachers replaced. Two associate pastors (at different times) were dismissed under fraudulent charges which she had trumped up—for no other reason than she felt threatened by their popularity. She and the pastor were in charge of all church finances. She endorsed the church checks. She was the power in that church and she manipulated her husband to work her will. This story could be repeated many times over—in many different churches.

The Apostle Paul says that racial, socioeconomic, and gender differences are abolished in Christ. This is certainly true in principle but all three concerns are alive and active in the shadow of the church. Among other things, this indicates that in the church we are quite elementary in our understanding of, capacity for, and practice of community. (More about this in chapters eight and nine.) Further, it illustrates that for the most part we are still only comfortable with those who are *like us*, whatever like us happens to be.

Part Three:

SHADOWBOXING (1)
THE INDIVIDUAL SHADOW

*It is easier, I know, to be neurotic. It is
easier to be parasitic. It is easier to relax
in the embracing arms of The Average.
Easier, but not better.*[1]

—Eugene Peterson

CHAPTER 6

Fighting the Good Fight

When I was a boy, Mohammed Ali (then known by
his birth name of Cassius Clay) fought the champion, Sonny
Liston, for the heavyweight championship of the world. The
year was 1964. I remember clearly watching this fight on
TV with my father. Several rounds into the fight Liston was
knocked down, and out, by one of the all-time famous
punches in boxing. The punch was as controversial as it was
renowned and for this reason—upon different slow motion
replays it appeared that Clay's "punch" did not connect with
Liston's jaw at all. In fact, it seemed to have missed him
completely. This, perhaps the most famous and controversial punch ever thrown in boxing, was even given a
name—the phantom punch.

This anecdote raises a vital issue. Are we actively engaged in confrontation with our shadow, or are we merely
throwing phantom punches? Another way of posing this
question is to ask, "Are we energetically and consciously pursuing psychospiritual growth, or are we lazily meandering
our way through life?" This question is important. It has a
great deal to do with the quality and significance of the life

---

[1] Eugene H. Peterson, *Run With the Horses* (InterVarsity Press, 1983), 18.

you and I lead and the impact of that life on those around us. It is a question deserving—in the quietness of our own soul and before God—the deepest reflection of which we are capable.

In this chapter, I want to describe the kind of activity we are called to be engaged in with our personal shadow.[1] From his own writings, we are fortunate that we can use as our model and example one of the most historically significant individuals of all time—the Apostle Paul.

While it would perhaps be an error to equate the two concepts, there is a definite ligature between the Jungian concept of shadow and the New Testament idea of that which the Apostle Paul terms "the old self" and "the sinful nature." The Bible characterizes the sinful nature as being lawless (Rom. 1:18-3:20) and succinctly defines sin as lawlessness (1 Jn. 3:4). This is an idea completely compatible with Jung who recognized this bent toward lawlessness in each human heart. It is precisely this Jung has in mind when he speaks of the statistical criminal residing in each of us. In Jung's words, "Everyone harbors his statistical criminal within himself."

No doubt some readers will balk at the idea that they possess a sinful side or a *statistical criminal* which they need to confront. A lot of time has been spent in pop-psych books over the last twenty years trying to assure us that we are all *okay*. There is a large and eager market for this message and why not? It feels pretty good to be told that you are fine just as you are.

As soothing as this message is, however, the fact is that there is a great deal about us that simply is not okay. I would call us back once again to the words of Jung; we stand as individuals in need of redemption. If we are unconscious of this basic truth about ourselves perhaps we are in the most

---

[1] Chapters eight and nine will deal with confronting the organizational shadow.

dangerous plight of all. We are as delusional as the group of people to whom Jesus directed the following story:

> [Jesus] told his next story to some who were complacently pleased with themselves over their moral performance and looked down their noses at the common people: "Two men went up to the Temple to pray, one a Pharisee, the other a tax man. The Pharisee posed and prayed like this: 'Oh, God, I thank you that I am not like other people—robbers, crooks, adulterers, or, heaven forbid, like this tax man. I fast twice a week and tithe on all my income.'
>
> "Meanwhile the tax man, slumped in the shadows, his face in his hands, not daring to look up, said, 'God, give mercy. Forgive me, a sinner.'"
>
> Jesus commented, "This tax man, not the other, went home made right with God. If you walk around with your nose in the air, you're simply going to end up flat on your face, but if you're content to be simply yourself, you will become more than yourself."[1]

How are we to go about the business of confronting our personal shadow? The seventh chapter of the Epistle to the Romans gives an excellent example of someone, the Apostle Paul, describing in revealing, frank, and transparent detail his struggle with the shadow. Actually, the word struggle is too anemic. Paul describes this activity as *warfare*. And this is the good fight that all and each of us is called to fight.

The Apostle was aware of his "dark brother," to use Jung's term, and saw in it a combatant against which he must strive if he is to gain spiritual growth and wholeness, that is, individuation. You can sense the angst in his words as Paul reports the raging *war* (his word) that is taking place

---

[1] Luke 18:9-14, *THE MESSAGE*.

within him. In fact, verses 14-15 of the seventh chapter of Romans could accurately be titled *Angst in Action.*

In this autobiographical snippet Paul discloses essential material about the shadow. Moreover, he illustrates for us firsthand what confrontation with the shadow is like. It is as though we have a crack journalist on the scene describing the battle in vivid detail for us who is at once engaged in the combat himself. To say the least, the shadow is a capable and crafty foe.

Paul writes:

> We know that the law [principles for living] is spiritual; but I am unspiritual, sold as a slave to sin. I do not understand what I do. For what I want to do I do not do, but what I hate I do. And if I do what I do not want to do, I agree that the law is good. As it is, it is no longer I myself who do it, but it is sin living in me. I know that nothing good lives in me, that is, in my sinful nature. For I have the desire to do what is good, but I cannot carry it out. For what I do is not the good I want to do; no, the evil I do not want to do—this I keep on doing. Now if I do what I no longer want to do, it is no longer I who do it, but it is sin living in me that does it.
>
> So I find this law [principle] at work: When I want to do good, evil is right there with me. For in my inner being I delight in God's law; but I see another law at work in the members of my body, waging war against the law of my mind and making me a prisoner of the law of sin at work within my members. What a wretched man I am! Who will rescue me from this body of death? Thanks be to God—through Jesus Christ our Lord!
>
> So then, I myself in my mind am a slave to God's law, but in the sinful nature a slave to the law of sin.

There was a pervasive, ongoing tension in Paul's life between his true[1] or spiritual Self and his shadow self or old nature. By the time Paul wrote this epistle he had been earnestly pursuing his spiritual development for many years, yet the battle continued. Paul had not *arrived*. Why is this so? Because the shadow is ever with us. Proportionally we may diminish its stature, we may see it grow weaker in its power and control as we grow toward individuation, but we will not eradicate it. Nor should we want to. This is a great mystery about which more will be said shortly.

Paul cuts right to the core of what fighting the good fight is all about. On behalf of the friends to whom he is writing Paul poses a rhetorical question to himself: "I know that all God's commands are spiritual, but I'm not. Isn't this also your experience?" "Yes," Paul replies. "I'm full of myself." He goes on to add:

> What I don't understand about myself is that I decide one way, but then I act another, doing things I absolutely despise. . . . I realize that I don't have what it takes. I can will it, but I can't *do* it. I decide to do good, but I don't *really* do it; I decide not to do bad, but then I do it anyway. My decisions, such as they are, don't result in actions. Something has gone wrong deep within me and gets the better of me every time.
>
> It happens so regularly that it's predictable. The moment I decide to do good, sin is there to trip me up. I truly delight in God's commands but it's obvious that not all of me joins in that delight. Parts of me covertly rebel, and just when I least expect it, they take charge.[2]

---

[1] *True self* is not used here to imply that the spiritual self is genuine while the ego-self or shadow-self is *false* or not really a part of us. Rather, by true self I mean to imply the Self that we are created to be—embracing and pursuing our uniqueness and psychospiritual growth. For clarity, when referring to the true self, I have chosen to capitalize the word, thus "Self."

[2] Rom. 7:14-23, *THE MESSAGE.*

Do you see it? "Something has gone wrong deep within me," Paul says. This is the warfare—recorded for us by the autobiographical pen of a great man—that is the common experience of all who pursue their spiritual development. Notice the extent of Paul's warfare. It affected and involved his spirit, mind, will, and emotions. If his words fail to strike a sympathetic chord deep within us, then we simply are not engaged in the walk of life. This deserves further elaboration.

When someone first purposes to pursue his psychospiritual development there is usually a brief elation and enthusiasm (a few days, a couple of weeks) followed hard after by a predictable sequence: first frustration, then confusion, then a sense of failure, followed by depression, then despair. It's very simple. He has just commenced a civil war—with himself. I always warn initiates into the walk of life to beware of this because it is inevitable. But they just do not get it at first. I understand their state of mind. This was my experience and it has been the experience of every man and woman on the walk of life.

In the early days and weeks, after one has committed herself to the journey, the elation and sense of gladness is such that the beginner simply cannot imagine this happening to her. Having finally given heed to that great inner voice there is such joy, such relief—such a glorious feeling of having surrendered to that which the thirsting soul so long has craved—she can never imagine this bliss being interrupted.

On more than one occasion I have warned a spiritual newborn as to what lies ahead but he simply cannot believe this will be *his* experience. Many times over initiates into the walk have said to me "I'm sure that happens to some people and I believe you. But I don't think it will happen to me. this is exactly what I have been longing for." He cannot be persuaded that there is a very real part of him that, like

Paul, has not and does not long for this at all! At that point there is nothing more that one can do save wait until the inevitable happens—don't worry, it will not take long—and be there to help him when it does.

An early source of confusion for young seekers is how suddenly their life is thrown into a chaos and a conflict that they never before knew nor dreamed of. This is the time you can share with them not only from Paul's explanation but from your own experience as well. They will be as ready for your words now as they were incredulous to them just a few days before.

With the pure confusion of a child—and we all begin to walk as children—she will say, "But I don't get it. My husband (parents, neighbor, etc.) isn't committed to his spiritual life at all and he isn't walking all over himself and being torn in two like I am. What am I doing wrong? This doesn't make sense." Ah, but it makes perfect sense.

Those who go through life living in the shadow—the old nature—are in a sense the living dead. There is no civil war within them at all. The Self, which is the battleground, the territory at stake, has been given over to the shadow. This explains the ease, on the existential level, of their lives. They show no battle fatigue because they are not at war. To these people, Paul's words sound like those of a madman—and so will yours. Let me explain.

The shadow is not subject to the principles of spiritual development. Further, it has no desire to be. (Recall Mr. Hyde's desire to avoid the light of day.) In fact, life in the shadow is the very antithesis of psychospiritual pursuit, that is, growth and development. This is precisely why I say that those who take no interest in their spiritual growth are the living dead. There is no spiritual life in them.

By its very nature, the unspiritual aspect of our self has no capacity for the spiritual life. It is not that the Spirit of God does not speak but rather that the unspiritual self has no desire to listen. It is not until we have committed to the road to spiritual development that we have an appetite to hear what the Spirit of God is saying to the living spirit within us. And so this is why there is no war taking place within those who are spiritually dead.

Interestingly, we have an incident from Paul's life proving this very point. While he was discussing the matters that are before us here with some Epicurean and Stoic intellectuals in Athens, these men became irritated with Paul. Muttering among themselves they asked, "What is this babbler trying to say?"[1] An accurate rendering of their question in today's vernacular would be, "What in the world is this idiot talking about?"

Jesus spoke to a crowd of such people one day and fared no better in terms of their assessment of him than Paul did, or we do. They thought he was nuts. If this sounds harsh it is not the worst of it. Some actually accused him of being in league with the devil! "He is demon-possessed and raving mad. Why listen to him?" they said.[2]

Returning now to the larger subject, the beginner must learn and the seasoned traveler must never forget that the spiritual life is a life of warfare. There are battles to be fought daily, for the shadow is a kind of lifeless vacuum that would ever draw us backwards. Mercifully, we are not without support in this battle nor are we without a strategy. (The issue of our support is of such significance that the entire final section of the book is given to it.) In the remainder of this chapter we will be exploring the strategy or battle plan which we must utilize if we are to conquer and subdue our personal shadow and bring it under control. First, some brief words about what we are *not* to do.

---

[1] Acts 17:18.
[2] John 10:19.

What is the solution to the question of the shadow? As I said earlier, the answer does not lie in attempting to eradicate the shadow. This is neither possible nor desirable. As Jung has pointed out to us, a person without a shadow would be nothing more than a two-dimensional phantom. Further, *the shadow is always telling us the truth about ourselves*, whether one likes to hear what it has to say or not. Listen to what John Sanford tells us about this important fact:

> The shadow . . . lies much closer to the Self than the egocentric ego does. No matter how outrageous the shadow might be, it is genuine, where the egocentric ego is not. The shadow has great energy precisely for this reason: in its genuiness it is in touch with the Self, the source of our psychic energy. The shocking fact is that in a showdown between the egocentric ego and the shadow the Self favors the shadow, even if it means the ego's eventual destruction.[1]

Just as the solution lies not in the effort to eradicate or extinguish the shadow, neither is the answer to be found in the unhealthy attempt to either suppress or repress it.[2] In fact, Jung equated trying to resolve the shadow question through psychological suppression with attempting to dispel a headache by lopping off the head!

The strategy for encountering the shadow is a threefold approach. It involves the metamorphosis of the mind, the principle of life as sacrament, and cultural resistance.

---

[1] John A. Sanford, *The Strange Trial of Mr. Hyde*, 138-139.

[2] In the context of shadow, Jung provides the following definitions of suppression and repression: "Suppression amounts to a conscious moral choice, but repression is a rather immoral 'penchant' for getting rid of disagreeable decisions." *The Collected Works of C. G. Jung*, vol. 11, *Psychology and Religion: West and East*, 75. Repression is an activity of the unconscious while suppression is a function of the conscious mind.

Metamorphosis of the Mind

The answer for dealing with the shadow begins with first raising the content of the shadow to the level of consciousness. This, Jung believed, is accomplished by means of thorough self-examination or self-analysis. St. Paul gives it to us like this: "Do not conform any longer to the pattern of this world, but be transformed *by the renewing of your mind.*[1] (emphasis added)

What is "the pattern of this world?" It is the shadow life. It is living in and for the old nature with no thought for the life of the spirit and psychospiritual development. In short, it is unconscious living. How are we to break free from this type of living? By having our mind *renewed.* A renewed mind is a conscious mind. It is alert to our higher purpose—that calling to spiritual growth. This is where we must begin. The self-examination Jung rightly calls for (incidently, so does Paul[2]) begins with a renewed mind, that is, a mind come to consciousness.

I recall a line by the lead female character in the movie *Joe Versus the Volcano.* Paraphrasing her words, she says: *My father says that the problem with the world is that most of the people travel through life fast asleep. But to those who are awake, life is an ever-unfolding miracle.* This is exactly so. The planet is inhabited by people who spend their days unconscious and oblivious to the greater mysteries of it all. They are on the world but not in it. They are fast asleep.

The strategy for fighting the good fight begins with the birth of a new mind within us (How can there be life without birth?). We have to have our eyes opened that we might see. On more occasions than one our Lord performed the miracle of restoring sight to the blind. This is a metaphor to illustrate that we each need to have our spiritual

---

[1] Rom. 12:2.
[2] 2 Cor. 13:5.

eyes opened. He chided the shadow-dwellers of his day for being blind to spiritual realities saying "Having eyes, do you not see?" And Paul says that if we do not "see" our spiritual calling it is because we only have eyes for "the fashionable god of darkness."[1]

In terms of shadow work, the way to the renewed mind, the mind come to consciousness, is through learning to dialogue with our shadow. This is the self-analysis Jung is speaking of.[2] Through this internal dialogue we become aware (conscious) of our shadow content. In short, that which was formerly unconscious is now lifted into consciousness—brought out into the light, as it were, where it can be engaged.[3]

Life As Sacrament

The second step in successfully combating the shadow embraces the principle that we might call *life as sacrament*. We are called to be living symbols of the fact that life is a sacred thing. Listen to these words: "So here's what I want you to do, God helping you: Take your everyday, ordinary life—your sleeping, eating, going-to-work, and walking-around life—and place it before God as an offering."[4] This is not only our calling but our high privilege as well. Remember this: If your life is not a sacrament then it must, of necessity, be profane.

A British army officer who was imprisoned with the Lutheran pastor and theologian Dietrich Bonhoeffer in the Gestapo prison at Flossenburg said of him: "Bonhoeffer always seemed to me to spread an atmosphere of happiness and joy

---

[1] 2 Cor. 4:4, *THE MESSAGE.*

[2] Freud tells us that the purpose of psychotherapy is to make the unconscious conscious.

[3] Two aids to this process are involvement in redemptive community and prayer (we will examine these in detail later in the book).

[4] Rom. 12:1, *THE MESSAGE.*

over the least incident and profound gratitude for the mere fact that he was alive. . . . He was one of the very few persons I have ever met for whom God was real and always near." That is life as sacrament. (Bonhoeffer was hanged by the Nazis, on special order from Heinrich Himmler, April 9, 1945. Days later, the Allies liberated the concentration camp at Flossenburg. He was 39 years old.)

Life as sacrament is a truth which we are just now beginning to reclaim from the seventeenth-century error that has reeked so much havoc. Remember, that is when the understanding was reached between science and religion to capriciously sever life down the middle, dividing it into the "natural" and the "spiritual" realms. This sacred/secular dichotomous nightmare has rent a garment that God intended to be whole and of a piece—and that is our life. As we saw earlier, life as sacrament was the crowning dignity that was present in the garden.

I believe that most of the social ills discussed in chapter one are the direct result of the loss of this truth. This is precisely how a people act when life has lost its majesty, its dignity—when living is no longer a sacramental act.

Still buying into the Enlightenment error, we erroneously believe that worship, praying, devotional reading, church attendance and the like are "spiritual activities" which are quite distinct from the "real life" issues of work and play, family and friends, and so on. We should listen again to Paul's words: "So here's what I want you to do, God helping you: Take your everyday, ordinary life—your sleeping, eating, going-to-work, and walking-around life—and place it before God as an offering." Nothing churchy about any of these things. This is the truth that we simply *must* reclaim. Life, all of life, is to be lived as sacrament. It is to be a living gift, offered up unto God. This is our high privilege and our need. It is the only thing that will prevent us from "collapsing in on ourselves" in spiritual darkness and social decay.

H. L. Mencken once wrote: "The basic fact about human existence is not that it is a tragedy, but that it is a bore. It is not so much a war as an endless standing in line." You know what; Mencken is absolutely correct . . . with one addition. This is precisely what life is like when it is not viewed and lived as sacrament. Mencken is giving a perfect description of the profane life.

Can you imagine the immediate change we would see if we all awoke tomorrow to the reality of life as sacrament? The practical—because this is an intensely practical issue—benefits would be staggering. Your car would actually come back from the garage properly repaired, because the mechanic would have considered his labors an act of worship. The Queen Anne chair you just purchased would last not only for your lifetime but that of your children's children as well. Why? Because the artisan who built it will revere her work as a sacrifice unto God. Realizing that your customers or clients are living offerings, as is your work, you would not dare overcharge them for your services. Children would not be wearing bulletproof vests to school. Their little lives are living sacraments. Who would dare harm them?

If this sounds to you a bit like the Puritan ethic you are right. For all their shortcomings (they too had a shadow to combat), the Puritans and their ethic have gotten a bad rap. Anyone who is a better student of history than of caricature knows this. At the very least, the Puritans recognized the truth of life as sacrament.

The shadow will resist you if you purpose to begin, by God's grace, to live out this truth. The shadow is lazy and narcissistic. Its greatest desire is to offer your life up as a sacrament to itself. This is all part of the battle.

Cultural Resistance

The third aspect of our strategy against the shadow is to realize that we must break free from the gravity of our culture, and then commit ourselves to doing so. "Don't become so well-adjusted to your culture that you fit into it without even thinking," Paul admonishes. We are back once again to unconsciousness—"without even thinking."

To use C. S. Lewis's marvelous expression, we dwell in the *Shadowlands*. If we are moving in lock-step with our culture we are in trouble. The walk of life rarely travels in the same direction as the world around it. Why is this? Because just like the shadow, culture is loaded with infantile fantasies—the very thing psychospiritual growth leads us out of. Furthermore, if the walk of life traveled in the same direction of the surrounding culture there would be no challenge. There would be no conflict. Vice-President Al Gore addresses this in his book *Earth in the Balance* when he says:

> We are monumentally distracted by a pervasive technological culture that appears to have a life of its own, one that insists on our full attention, continually seducing us and pulling us away from the opportunity to experience directly the true meaning of our own lives.

The majority of people who have lived in this world have shown neither interest nor appetite for pursuing their spiritual growth. I do not mean to imply that they are categorically malevolent people. Typically, such people are just concerned with the matters of day-to-day existence and are, as I said earlier, just lazily meandering their way through life.

The American culture the seeker of the spiritual life will find facing her is immature and banal—infantile. Perhaps the most salient analysis of our cultural I have ever read is from Eugene Peterson. Quoting him at length, he writes:

> The puzzle is why so many people live so badly. Not so wickedly, but so inanely. Not so cruelly, but so stu-

pidly. There is little to admire and less to imitate in the people who are prominent in our culture. We have celebrities but not saints. Famous entertainers amuse a nation of bored insomniacs. Infamous criminals act our the aggressions of timid conformists. Petulant and spoiled athletes play games vicariously for lazy and apathetic spectators. People, aimless and bored, amuse themselves with trivia and trash. Neither the adventure of goodness nor the pursuit of righteousness gets headlines.

Modern man is "a bleak business," says Tom Howard. "To our chagrin we discover that the declaration of autonomy has issued not in a race of free masterly men, but rather in a race that can be described by its poets and dramatists only as bored, vexed, frantic, embittered, and sniffling."

This condition has produced an odd phenomenon: individuals who live trivial lives and then engage in evil acts in order to establish significance for themselves. Assassins and hijackers attempt the gigantic leap from obscurity to fame by killing a prominent person or endangering the lives of an airplane full of passengers. Often they are successful. The mass media report their words and display their actions. Writers vie with one another in analyzing their motives and providing psychological profiles on them. No other culture has been as eager to reward either nonsense or wickedness.

If, on the other hand, we look around for what it means to be a mature, whole, blessed person, we don't find much. These people are around, maybe as many of them as ever, but they aren't easy to pick out. No journalist interviews them. No talk show features them. They are not admired. They are not looked up to. They do not set trends. There is no cash value in them. No Oscars are given for integrity. At year's end no one compiles a list of the ten best-lived lives.[1]

---

[1] Eugene H. Peterson, *Run With the Horses,* 11-12. On the subject of psychospiritual growth, this is easily one of the best books I have read.

In his rich translation of the New Testament, J. B. Phillips gives it to us like this: "Don't let the world around you squeeze you into its mold."[1] With all the talk of individuality we hear, the fact of the matter is that society is quite intolerant of those who do not simply go with the popular flow. Like any pathological system, society pressures its members to maintain the equilibrium of the system—even if that equilibrium is most unhealthy. We must remember that we are called to move out of the shadow. We are called to pursue psychospiritual development. The unfortunate fact is, if we relax and move with the flow of our culture, it will end up dragging us down to its level of immaturity, just as we are warned. Our culture has a way of dulling one's touch with the sacred center of his life.

To the contrary, God wants to develop well-formed maturity in us, as he leads us down the path of individuation. This is utterly impossible if we march, like proverbial lemmings to the sea, in lockstep with our culture.

This fact does not mean we are to abandon our world. Not at all. It simply recognizes that if we are going to be the "light of the world" we ourselves cannot be immersed in darkness. If we are going to be the "salt of the earth" we cannot ourselves be without flavor. It is only when—in the proper sense—we are not immersed in our culture that we have anything of value to offer it.

So then, this is the strategy we are to deploy as we fight the good fight against our shadow in the pursuit of psychospiritual growth and advancement. We must, through the renewing of our mind, raise the content of our shadow to consciousness. Indeed, the renewed mind is, if I may say it this way, *nothing more* than coming to consciousness. We are called to consciousness of ourselves (shadow work), of

---

[1] Rom 12:2 in J. B. Phillips, *The New Testament in Modern English* (Geoffrey Bles, 1963).

our vocation to psychospiritual development, of spiritual realities, of social responsibility, and consciousness of God. The second component of our strategy is the reality of life as sacrament. If we are not convinced in the marrow of our being of this truth, we will either fail to engage the fight or somewhere along the way we will give up. Why is fighting the good fight worth it? Because the living sacrifice (our "everyday, ordinary life") we offer up must be something more than the swill of a shadowy, unconscious existence.

The final aspect of our strategy against the shadow is the necessity of cultural resistance. This is in essence an ideological issue. The values, attitudes, and mind set of popular culture are ideologically different than those which lead to psychospiritual development. The surrounding culture, as I said earlier, can dull our touch with the sacred center of our lives. This is why saints have always viewed themselves as transients in their culture.

We live in the Shadowlands. The driving force behind our culture is the shadow, the old nature. Logically, we will find no ally against our shadow here. We must strive for that delicate balance of being fully *in* the world while at the same time not being *of* it. That is to say, not sharing in the fundamental approach to life embraced by our culture as a whole.

I return again to the question raised at the outset of this chapter. Are we actively engaged in warfare with our shadow—what could truly be called shadowboxing—or are we merely throwing phantom punches at our own lack of psychospiritual development under the pretense of engagement? I cannot answer that question for you, just as you cannot for me. But it is vitally important that we each address this question—address it, and answer it honestly.

My strength is as the strength of ten,
Because my heart is pure.[1]
—Alfred, Lord Tennyson

CHAPTER 7

Mariah: The Example of a Warrior

While away working on this book I had an encounter that was wonderfully serendipitous. I had been writing for some time in the little out-of-the-way town where I often go to write, and decided to take a break and walk downtown. I went into a small shop to browse about and quite unintentionally got into a conversation with the manager—a forty-two year old wonder named Mariah, whose personal story is one of the most astounding I have ever heard.

After our initial conversation I arranged with Mariah to take her to lunch the next day so that I might tape-record her story more fully and, with her permission, share it with you, the reader. Mariah is a warrior. She is a living example of what it means to fight the good fight.

Mariah was raised in a home with an alcoholic father who was also a moonshiner. Mariah's grandfather was also a moonshiner, as was his father before him. Concomitant with all the craziness alcoholism brings to a family, Mariah's family was also dirt poor. Forget normal, her early years were barely

---

[1] Tennyson, Alfred, Lord, "Sir Galahad" in *The Poems and Plays of Alfred Lord Tennyson* (Random House, 1938), 189.

survivable. Mariah was legally blind until her school years. At that time she had ocular surgery which allowed her for the first time to see properly.

At the age of nine the pattern of behavior began which, sadly, often completes the circle in the type of family background that Mariah had. This behavior is one of the most tragic and psychologically destructive things that a child can experience. Mariah became the victim of sexual abuse. The devastation was compounded by the fact that the perpetrator was her own biological father. In a drunken state he would call her to himself and fondle her—his sordid pleasure at her ghastly expense. Mariah was subject to this kind of treatment for about three years.

Mariah married young. She wanted to get away from home. But she escaped the frying pan only to land squarely in the fire. It was a desperate girl's desperate act. Mariah's husband was from a family that was primitive, wild. They were uneducated and unrefined mountain people.

It did not take long for the luster to wear off of this young marriage. Bill, Mariah's husband, got heavily involved with drug use and soon, drug dealing. Before long, Bill was a major player in the drug traffic in the area. He was soon handling mass quantities of dope and was fortifying his connections to some of the most powerful and dangerous players in the drug underworld. Mariah hated what was going on at her house. She did not like being around his drug buddies.

Then came the verbal and physical violence. It was mild at first, judging by the level to which it would later intensify. There was pushing and shoving, outbursts of anger, verbal attacks. Like the early drug involvement, this was only to be the beginning of the nightmare. Before long the treatment would evolve into torture. Her life would become hellish.

Like the flowers that grew in Flanders fields, two beautiful children were born into the chaos of this war zone. How to shield them from the violence? This was Mariah's ever-growing burden.

Bill's behavior became increasingly depraved, his treatment of Mariah increasingly cruel. Then there came the inflicting of a pain whose bruises are just as real albeit invisible to the eye. His vow to her became a joke. Bill slept with whomever he wished. Pitifully, Mariah's own family added to her chaos. Two of her sisters—her own blood sisters—were having sex with Bill, she would come to learn.

I earlier referred to the treatment Mariah received from her husband's own hands as torture. The word is neither extreme nor melodramatic. It is accurate. What follows is a partial account of what she endured.

Coming home in a fit of rage one evening, Bill turned his fury on Mariah. Precariously, she was in the bathtub at the time. Jerking her by the hair, he crammed her head into the water. He held her there, underwater, until she blacked out.

When he was in the throes of his anger, whatever Bill had in his hands became a weapon. He would not hesitate to use anything he could grab when he was ready to attack. On three separate occasions Mariah was stabbed by her husband. Twice, the weapon of choice was a knife. The other time he used a kitchen fork.

Then there was the time an argument broke out in the bedroom. One of many such times. But this one ended in a way that was vivid even by the standards of Bill's behavior. He struck Mariah in the face with the butt of a pistol. Her jaw was shattered.

I mentioned that Bill was having sex with two of Mariah's own sisters. Mariah walked into her house one day to find him in bed with one of them. She could not believe her eyes. Outraged, she verbally launched into both of them. Her weapons were words. Bill retaliated, only not in kind. He chose a different weapon. In the corner of the bedroom stood a rifle. Bill grabbed up the rifle and started toward Mariah with it. He raised the rifle as though he were in combat attacking the enemy. He struck Mariah a severe blow in the neck with the rifle butt. Her cervical vertebrae were cracked.

When hearing of such domestic violence people will inevitably ask, "Why didn't you just leave?" This reveals a gross ignorance of the dynamics of domestic violence, particularly when the perpetrator is as violent as Mariah's husband. Fleeing often results in the victim being hunted down like an animal by the perpetrator—and only intensifies the abuse. The same occurs when the abuser is reported to the authorities. This is why so many accounts of spouse and child abuse go unreported. Mariah's case illustrates this fact. On two or three occasions she tried to leave Bill, taking her children and going to her parents' house. Bill would physically retrieve her, then beat her for having left. (One can only imagine what violence those children must have been witness to throughout their young lives.) Further, Bill warned Mariah that if she should ever take the children and leave the area, he would kill her parents by dynamiting their home.

Bill would come home, meet Mariah at the door and for no other reason than the fact that she was handy, punch her out. In her own words, "You've heard of people who would get mad and kick the dog? We [Mariah and the children] were his dogs."

Mariah had been choked more times than she could count or remember. And bruises were as common as headaches.

The End . . . The Beginning

One fateful day in June everything came to a head. Mariah discovered to her horror that her daughter, then eleven, was being molested by Bill's best friend. (She was later to discover that the molestation had recurred repeatedly over a four to five year period. Later, to her continued horror, she would find out that her husband—their daughter's biological father, would sit by and watch his friend ravage his own daughter.) Mariah vividly remembers crying out to God: "Lord. That's it. I have taken a lot but I can't take this."

Mariah went to her mother-in-law and told her what had taken place. As any therapist can tell you, the woman's response was sick, but not atypical. "You had better not tell a soul," she threatened. And this was happening to her own granddaughter![1]

When Mariah learned of the molestation of her daughter she confronted her husband. The events you are about to read took place just one day after Mariah's thirty-third birthday. At this point, I am going to use Mariah's own words to tell you the final chapter of this horror story.

I told Bill "this is it. I'm not afraid of you anymore. I don't care what you do." I told him that I was going to the Department of Family and Children Services and report his friend and then I was going to the police to swear a warrant for his [the friend's] arrest. Then, I told him, I was going to file for a divorce. I had had it.

Bill went nuts. He pulled a pistol from the back of his pants and started pistol-whipping me. I fell back onto the floor. I was laying there half conscious. I thought I heard a mouse. It was my daughter in the living room crying. I came fully to and ran to the room. Bill was straddled across our daughter's lap, fist-whipping her with both hands in the face. Our son would cry and Bill would backhand him.[2]

---

[1] Later, the grandmother would let this same man come to her house when Mariah's two children were visiting there. Mariah was outraged when she learned of this. She managed to have the paternal grandparents' visitation rights revoked.

[2] The daughter was 11 at the time, the son was six.

In a rush of pure adrenalin I ran to Bill and, picking him up from behind off of my daughter, I threw him across the room into the kitchen like he was a teddy bear. (He was about six feet tall and weighed just over 200 pounds. I weighed about 130 pounds.) I always told the kids that if there father ever killed me they were to take hands and run for their lives. I always expected that he would kill me and I figured this would be the time. But I didn't care. I was no longer afraid.

We fought all over that kitchen. When I could break away I would try to grab the kids and run away. I couldn't get them to the door before he would knock me down and literally pick up my kids and throw them back on the other side of the room. This happened two or three times.

We ended up back in the kitchen somehow. We fought all over that kitchen. Bill kept a .38 caliber "Saturday night special" on a cabinet in the kitchen. He grabbed the pistol and pointed it right between my eyes. He screamed, "Damn you bitch; I'm going to kill you! I'm going to kill you, and then I'm going to kill the kids, and then I'm going to kill myself! Because when everybody finds out about all of this they are going to blame me!"

He kept saying this over and over. I kept saying to him, "It *is* your fault, it *is* your fault!" All through the years I never talked back. I was always afraid. I took the beatings. Every time I had ever tried to open my mouth I got it busted. But no more. I figured this would be the day I would die but I had run out of fear. I remember saying to myself, "If I am going to die then damn it, let this be the day. I'm not going to take it anymore." Something just said to me, "If I'm going to die today, then I'm going to go down fighting."

I remember hitting the gun and it knocked it out of his hand and I kicked it away. Then I remember trying to get to my kids again and he grabbed me by the hair of the head and pulled me down to the kitchen floor and we fought and fought.

Somehow I got the gun in my hand, I don't remember how. I remember hearing a shot and I figured I had been shot because we both had hold of the gun and were struggling for it. But I didn't feel anything. He fell. When it all ended he had been shot five times. The police said I had emptied the gun in him after he fell. I don't even remember that but that's what they said. They said the first shot severed the aorta in the chest. Then he was shot in the abdomen, the upper leg, the lower leg, and in the arm. The police said I evidently shut my eyes and just fired. There was no aim, no pattern, nothing. They said one shot hit the wall.

Me and my kids were so beat up; we were so beat up. He kept crawling toward us with five bullets in him saying, "I'm gonna kill you all, I'm gonna kill you all, I'm gonna kill you all."[1]

I don't remember shooting five times. When the police asked me how many times I shot him I said "I remembered hearing one shot and I thought I heard another but I really don't remember."

The kids saw all of this. While he was crawling toward me after being shot five times I screamed to the kids, "Kids run! Run! Run!" I didn't know how many times he was shot or how bad he was hurt because he kept crawling toward me, toward the door.

I remember walking out onto the porch and saying to [my neighbor], "Call an ambulance and call the police." He had stopped crawling and he had collapsed.

The police, people, everybody came. I remembered more things later that I didn't remember right at the time. The first police officer on the scene had been to our house

---

[1] At this point Mariah referred to something which would begin shortly after this fateful day saying "Do you see why my kids were in therapy for two years?"

several times because of domestic violence. He later told me that when he got there I was sitting in the yard with the empty gun still in my hand. I don't remember this. I guess I was in shock. He said he came over to me and I told him I had shot Bill. He asked for the gun and said that I held my arm out to him but didn't release the gun. He said he couldn't get it out of my hand. He was a heavy-set guy but he said it took all he could do to pry the gun out of my hand.

The officer picked me up, put me on the porch, and went in the house. He told me to sit there and he would be right back. When he came back I asked him if Bill was dead. He said, "It's alright. Don't worry about it."

About that time a car came sliding in the driveway sideways. It was Bill's brother. He just happened to be coming by, on his way home from work. He went in and saw his dead brother and ran out trying to attack me. The officer pushed him off and locked me in his police car. He placed a guard with me, another officer, to protect me and to keep Bill's family and friends who were now there from killing me. The sheriff and an agent from the [state] Bureau of Investigation got in the car with me. (Mariah later found out that the [state] Bureau of Investigation had their house under surveillance for some time because of all the drug activity Bill was involved in. In Mariah's words, "They knew what was going on.")

I was taken to the Sheriff's Department for questioning and the children were taken to the Department of Human Services for the same. Later that evening, my children were taken to my mother.

Riding down the road the sheriff said I didn't have to answer any questions without a lawyer if I didn't want to, but if I wanted to voluntarily do so I could tell him what happened. I said, "I can't tell a lawyer anything different from what I would tell you. All I can tell is what happened." He knew I was telling the truth. The investigation of the house, where the whole incident occurred, backed me up. Plus, they knew some of the history.

I was taken to the Sheriff's Department and they took a lot of pictures. They weren't mug shots. They were taking pictures of my body. I had both lips cut open and my nose was broken. My eyes were almost beaten shut. I looked like I had been in an eight-round fight or something. I had bruises all over me. This is why they took all the pictures. They took pictures of my children. My daughter's mouth was cut inside and out and her jaw was cut on the inside. Her teeth were bloody around the gums where they had been knocked loose. Her face was bruised and one of her jaw teeth was knocked out. I was all to pieces. I was in shock. I couldn't hardly walk. My head hurt so bad that I thought I was going to die. My head was absolutely killing me from all the blows.

They took my fingerprints and they took my statement. They asked me if I would ride with them and show them where Bill's marijuana patches were. (Bill also had a suitcase of drugs in the house when he was killed, which the [state] Bureau of Investigation found upon searching the house.) I did this, then they took me to my mother's. I was released without having to sign bail. Uncles, friends, people I had worked for in the past, all showed up to sign my bail because in trouble like this you have to do that. But I didn't have to post bail. In fact, there was never a trial because the police investigation later said that this was an act of self-defense.

It was just like—I don't know—it was just like you were in a plane crash or something. You walk out of it and you think, "God, I can't believe this has just happened to me." I didn't sleep for days. I couldn't rest; I couldn't sit down; I couldn't eat; I couldn't drink water. I couldn't hold anything on my stomach. I almost flipped out. It was just so devastating.

And then to have to go through the funeral. We couldn't go to the funeral. My sister-in-law took me and my children to the funeral home early in the morning when they had him prepared, before day-light. I took my kids in there and I said, "Kids, this is your daddy. In his own way he loved you. But he had problems he couldn't deal with." I said, "We were the things he took it out on."

This was not the end of Mariah's nightmare. She and her children had to be under police protection for more than a year after that tragic day in June to protect them from death threats made by Bill's family and his former drug associates. After the death of her husband Mariah had a total of twenty-three death threats made on her life.

Both children were in therapy for the two years proceeding the death of their father. For years to follow, Mariah would have to inspect the entire house every night to assure her daughter that the man who had molested her for those four to five years was not hiding in the house.[1] Mariah was many times awakened in the night by her daughter pounding on the foot of the bed, having been awakened out of a terrible nightmare. Mariah would hold her in her arms, up in the bed, until she fell asleep. To this day, and she is now a grown young lady, Mariah's daughter has nightmares that her father and his friend are after her.

Before visitation rights were taken away from the paternal grandparents, things would occur at their house that were destroying Mariah's children. She says:

At first they had my kids so screwed up. They took my kids to his grave and because the grave had settled, as all new graves do, they said "that's because your dad has

---

[1] The Sheriff's Department and the Department of Human Services obtained a full confession from the man. He was convicted of the crime and sentenced to 10 years in prison.

come out of his grave." Bill's parents told my kids that their dad had been seen near home and that they had seen him in the evening shadows. They are bonkers. They saw ghosts, heard voices. They were just the typical, illiterate, inbred mountain people. They would even allow the man who had been molesting my daughter to come to their house while my kids were there, I later found out. When he would show up, [my daughter] would crawl down in the space between the wall and the bed— terrified—waiting for him to leave.

The only good thing to come from this was that, armed with this horrendous information, the DHS therapist was able to legally have all grandparental visitation rights withdrawn.

Life was hard. To support herself and her children Mariah worked three jobs at one point. She would go early in the morning to the restaurant where she worked as a hostess. At midday, she would go to the hair salon where she worked as a beautician. She would then return in the evening to the restaurant and work late into the evening hours. Her mother helped out as she could by watching the children after school. Because of her long hours and hard work—and no doubt from the years of abuse she had heaped on her as well—Mariah began experiencing physical problems that are with her to this day.

Grace Abounding

It is now time to weave this deeply disturbing, practically unbelievable story into the theme of this chapter and into the fabric of this book as a whole. As I said at the outset, Mariah is a living example of what it means to fight the good fight.

Can you imagine anyone who has the material for more of a shadow than Mariah? Who among us could not understand if she were poisoned with hatred and bitterness, consumed with self-pity and starving for revenge? If she were fueled by repressed, unconscious, dark energy, who could blame her? It is almost as if she has a right to be human wreckage. But this is not Mariah.

Shortly after those tragic years came to a close, Mariah and her children began putting the pieces of their lives together. Mariah says that she believes there are three things it takes to do this.

"Number one," she says, "is that you have got to have a spiritual base." Listen very carefully to these words. After reading her story I'm sure that, like me, you believe Mariah has earned the right to be heard. She says, "I believe that there is spiritual healing. I believe that you have to have faith in God and ask help from him." Mariah continues:

> Next, you have got to believe in yourself. You have to be willing to receive the help God will give you and you have to be willing to do what it takes. I believe you have to have a will. You can't do anything if you don't have the will, the desire, the drive. I am a survivor. I believe in myself. No matter what it is I will be found climbing to the top.

Mariah sees her life as a sacrament. She believes that she is full of meaning and that God has a purpose for her. In the most spiritually healthy of ways, she believes in herself.

"Last, you have got to accept what life sends your way," she says. "You have to accept things as they are and then you have to do something about the things that you can," she adds. "You can't sit and whine and say 'Oh God, I'm this or I'm that, or why did this happen to me?' I don't know why this happened to me!"

Mariah is not without her demons—but they are for the most part *conscious* demons. Remember that Jung said the first step in overcoming the shadow is to raise its contents to consciousness by self-analysis. Mariah is aware of her issues. She is conscious of them. Listen to her comments.

They reveal a woman that is full of insight as to the dynamics taking place within her. She is not a shadow dweller:

> I had a lot of bitterness. I still have some. I fight it constantly. It is a constant battle to struggle against bitterness, and anger, and resentment. I forgive people who have done things to me and hurt me and then there would be a moment when my daughter would go through the terrible things she would go through and I would think "Oh damn him. Damn him for hurting her" (the guy that molested her daughter). But then I would think "No, you've got to pray for him and forgive him because some day he will get what's coming to him—someday he will." You don't get away with anything. Grandma used to say "Whatever goes under the horses belly eventually goes over its back." That means whatever you do "under the table" will eventually end up on the top. You don't get away with anything.

Mariah refused to give in to her dark side. It would have been easy to wallow but she refused to do that. She put herself through beautician school. She worked hard to provide for her family.

Mariah was aware of the truth of life as sacrament—and she practiced it. She said, "I figured one way to make some sense out of all the bad things that had happened to me was to let God use me to help other people." Mariah began working with local agencies to help battered women. She spoke to support groups and civic groups. She worked with law enforcement agencies, mental health professionals, and social services to give them an insider's view of domestic violence. She worked to get passage of stronger and better laws pertaining to child molesters. Mariah took her nightmare and presented it, as well as herself, up to God as a living offering.

Mariah continues to work hard to improve herself and to build into the lives of her children. She has taken some non-credit college courses at a local community college because in her words, "I want to improve myself." Both of her children are still at home with her. Her daughter is now twenty and her son is sixteen years old. Mariah says, "I have two best friends and they are my kids. We are like the Three Musketeers—it's all for one and one for all."

One thing that to me as a therapist shows particular insight is a practice Mariah has instituted for her family. What a great device for training her children in the ways of consciousness and leading them away from the shadowy, unconscious lifestyle. She says,

> The three of us sit around the table and air things out about every two weeks. We will deal with our issues and don't let them pile up. There are just two rules. You can say whatever you want and express whatever emotions you have but you have to respect the dignity of the other person. No angry physical contact of any kind is allowed.

Today, Mariah's daughter is working for her uncle and saving money to go to college. Her son has a summer job lined up once school is out. Both of Mariah's children are alcohol and drug free.

Mariah says, "When I get depressed I put on my jogging shoes and jog or workout. I talk to a friend, I do *something*. I don't allow myself to wallow. You have to have a strength within. You have to have an inner hero." Mariah knows how to do battle with the shadow. She knows what it is to fight the good fight. She is a modern day warrior.

Part Four:

SHADOWBOXING (2) -
THE
ORGANIZATIONAL
SHADOW

*In modern industrial society we often
purchase our material well-being at a high
human cost, the chief symptom of which is
the destruction of community.*[1]
—Daniel Yankelovich

CHAPTER 8

Understanding Community: The Five Stages

We now turn our attention to the engagement of the organizational or collective shadow. As the church was used to explore the concept of organizational shadow (chapter five), it is only logical that we use this same organization as we talk about confrontation of the collective shadow. (As a reminder let me say once again that any and every *organization*—all that is required is two or more people who are interrelated in some fashion—has a shadow to confront. If your courtship, your family, your business, is characterized by disharmony, chaos, strife, a lack of productivity, then you would be wise to investigate the collective shadow. Businesses and corporations, for example, suffer immensely in terms of dissonance among personnel and poor productivity when they fail to confront their shadow.)

In chapter nine I will address how the church is to confront and embrace its collective shadow through

---

[1] Daniel Yankelovich, *New Rules* (Random House, 1981), 226.

community. This is what we might call community practiced or community in action. However, application comes subsequent to understanding. It is therefore fitting that we seek to enlarge our understanding of community before discussing its application respective to the organizational shadow.[1]

There are stages of development in the life of a community. We are indebted to the excellent work of Scott Peck for his years of labor in, what we might call, the scientific investigation of community. Dr. Peck and his associates at FCE[2] have isolated four stages of community-making. While a number of different names have been given for these stages Peck calls them: pseudocommunity, chaos, emptiness, and community[3] or, what I prefer to call, redemptive community.

From my own experience with groups over the years, and the observations I have drawn from them, I have to add a fifth stage to the development of redemptive community—namely, conflict. For me then, the stages of true community-making are 1) pseudocommunity, 2) conflict, 3) chaos, 4) surrender (analogous to Peck's "emptiness"), and 5) redemptive community. As we are considering the importance of community relative to the organizational shadow as seen in the church, I will relate these stages to a church context.

---

[1] Of course, the practice of community is essential in dealing with the individual shadow as well.

[2] In 1984 Dr. Peck and others formed the Foundation for Community Encouragement, Inc., (FCE). FCE is a nonprofit, tax-exempt, public educational foundation. To find out more about FCE or support its worthy mission contact: The Foundation for Community Encouragement, PO Box 449, Ridgefield, Connecticut 06877, (203/431-9484).

[3] See M. Scott Peck, *The Different Drum: Community Making and Peace* (Simon & Schuster, Inc., 1987), 86-106.

PseudoCommunity

Stage one toward redemptive community is pseudocommunity. This is the stage of feigned community. It is characterized by pretense—what my grandmother used to refer to as "put-on." I do not *necessarily* mean to imply that this pretense is of a conscious, duplicitous intent. (Although I do believe that most of it is.)

There is also illusion at work here. Illusions are wish-based desires to manipulate reality (and will be discussed in more detail in chapter nine). I believe many well-intentioned people enter community in the throes of illusions as to what community is all about. If community proceeds, these illusions will somewhere along the way be shattered.

Listen to the insight Peck gives us about this initial stage toward community:

> The group pretends it already is a community, that the participants have only superficial individual differences and no cause for conflict. The primary means it uses to maintain this pretense is through a set of unspoken common norms we call manners: you should try your best not to say anything that might antagonize or upset anyone else; if someone else says something that offends you or evokes a painful feeling or memory, you should pretend it hasn't bothered you in the least; and if disagreement or other unpleasantness emerges, you should immediately change the subject. These are rules that any good hostess knows. They may create a smoothly functioning dinner party but nothing more significant. The communication in a pseudocommunity is filled with generalizations. It is polite, inauthentic, boring, sterile, and unproductive.[1]

---

[1] M. Scott Peck, *A World Waiting to be Born* (Bantam Books, 1993), 274.

Everything about pseudocommunity is phony. There is phony communication, phony unity, phony interest, phony goodness, phony psychospiritual development. It's all window dressing. Why is this? Peck hits it: "Beware of instant community. Community-making requires time as well as effort and sacrifice. It cannot be cheaply bought. . . . In pseudocommunity a group attempts to purchase community cheaply by pretense."[1] Pseudocommunity is as it is because basically, at this stage people are trying to get as much as possible for as little as possible.

I believe, God help us, that most churches never rise above the stage of pseudocommunity. This is why her shadow looms so large. Living in pseudocommunity, the church's shadow is never confronted.

Pseudocommunity is polite, inauthentic, boring, sterile, mundane, and unproductive. This is precisely how the church is too often described and, sadder, it is too often how church is experienced. In such a climate, little wonder that one who is spiritually parched can walk into church only to leave under the impression that he cannot find there that which his soul desires. Worn long enough the mask tends to become the face itself. This is as true for organizations as for individuals and may explain why the church often seems more like a Greek play—sometimes *comedy*, sometimes *tragedy*—than a vibrant spiritual community.

I recall reading a story in which a man was excitedly telephoned by a friend who wanted him to come to his house right away. Once the man arrived his friend said, "I have been working on something for months that I want you to see." He led the man down the hall and into a room in which he had constructed a large machine, square in the center of the room. He asked, "What do you think of it?"

"Impressive," the man responded, "did you build this?"

---

[1] M. Scott Peck, *The Different Drum*, 88.

"Sure did," his friend said, adding "but you haven't seen anything. Watch this." He then flipped a switch on the machine and the thing came alive with motion—wheels turning, gears churning, the hum of quiet efficiency.

"That's incredible," the man said, "what does it do?"

"Do?" his friend responded, "it doesn't *do* anything. But doesn't it run smoothly!"

That's pseudocommunity. It doesn't *do* anything. But it runs smoothly.

Conflict

The second stage in the growth toward redemptive community is conflict. If the group hangs together through the pseudocommunity, conflict is inevitable. Sooner or later a word of honesty will leak out or someone will act or speak out of their authentic Self (individuality), and the show is over. (The step to conflict can be facilitated by a skilled leader.) It's an hilarious thing to see, frankly. No more generalities, no more suppression of differences, and as for conflict-avoidance—well, it has just gone out the window!

In terms of the collective shadow and the church, when a church gets stuck in the conflict stage of community bad things happen. It is in the conflict stage that churches split. This is what happens: The pseudocommunity has evolved into the conflict stage. Rather than press on to and through the subsequent stages toward redemptive community, the people divide into (usually) two factions over some point of contention. Sometimes this just-under-the-surface conflict will remain, simmering for years and robbing that church of spiritual power. Usually what happens is a church split, the one becoming two. This is a sad but common story—as common as rain. We might not like to face it, but this points to the psychological immaturity of the people involved and how underdeveloped they are in terms of psychospiritual development.

111

(If you are a businessman or businesswoman and wonder why your company has stalled despite a good product, a good market niche, and the like, I would suggest your examine if you and your personnel are stuck in the conflict stage.)

Have you ever wondered why you can be with friends or family that you have not seen in a long time, perhaps years, and you have the most wonderful time together, rekindling the relationship, feeding off of each others presence. It's marvelous . . . for a while.

And then little things about them begin to annoy you, then irritate you, then infuriate you. (By the way, the same thing is simultaneously occurring in them.) You are experiencing the first rumblings of the transition from pseudocommunity to conflict. You have discovered experientially that old quip, "What do company and fish have in common? In three days they both stink!"

As awkward and painful as it is, conflict is not inherently a bad thing. Indeed, it is essential in the community-building process at this point. Otherwise, the group would not move beyond pseudocommunity and the whole mess would die of natural causes (actually, it would be a mercy killing). The conflict arises because our true selves are crying out "ENOUGH!" In the conflict stage the personalities sort of erupt through the thin surface of phony civility that is pseudocommunity in much the same way that steam escapes through fissures in the earth's crust.

When a group reaches the conflict stages things get interesting. Feelings that had been stirred by words that had been spoken earlier which hurt or annoyed or angered—feelings which were politely suppressed away—reappear, their robbed vigor restored. Suddenly, the group may be a lot of things, but it is no longer boring. At this point one of two things occurs (that is, if the group does not disband or split apart). Either the group will regress, returning once again to pseudocommunity, or it will proceed to the next stage.

Chaos

Conflict gives way to the next step in community-building and that is chaos. Let us back up for a moment. In pseudocommunity, uniformity (which is always superficial) was feigned. In the conflict stage individuality and, hence, differences surface. The phony consonance of pseudocommunity gives way to the dissonance of the conflict stage. Now, in the chaos stage, the energy goes toward restoring the consonance that existed prior to the rise of conflict.

In the church, this is where the verse-stamping which I referred to earlier kicks into high gear. The problems, obstacles, and differences that the group tried to ignore in stage one and that erupted in stage two are now in the open. This makes everyone feel a bit uncomfortable, a bit naked. In the rush to restore the old equilibrium *advice* is as common as air. In the church this advice is usually delivered in the form of verse-stamping.

Someone may confess to being worried over a straying child. Out of the pack will come "You know, God's Word says, 'I will keep him in perfect peace whose mind is fixed on me.'" Someone else may apologize to another member for having lashed out at her in anger. To which the humble forgiver will in turn reply, "That's okay. You just got in the flesh." And on and on it goes. The room is thick with answers. If someone who is not familiar with the lingo and games of the church happens to be in the group he just listens—thinking its all *bull* and that the whole lot of them are, at best, superficial—out of touch with any sort of hardy view of reality and human experience.

All of this has less to do with real communication than it does with nervous energy. The intent at this point is not really to build up one another, though the various members might think this is the case. The real motivation, as I have already said, is about dispelling the chaos, the confusion that is now in the air and restoring the previous equilibrium from stage one. Listen to Scott Peck's description of the chaos stage:

> The chaos always centers around well-intentioned but misguided attempts to heal and convert. . . .
>
> By and large, people resist change. So the healers and converters try harder to heal or convert, until finally their victims get their backs up and start trying to heal the healers and convert the converters. It is indeed chaos. . . .
>
> In the stage of chaos individual differences are, . . . right out in the open. Only now, instead of trying to hide or ignore them, the group is attempting to obliterate them. Underlying the attempts to heal and convert is not so much the motive of love as the motive to make everyone *normal*—and the motive to win, as the members fight over whose norm might prevail.[1]

I have known pastors—and entire churches—who think they have the answer to any question that can be raised. No matter how arcane, no matter how much mystery involved (I've even known people who could "explain" the doctrine of the Trinity!) they had an answer. This deeper knowledge does not come from superior insight but from the shadow. It emanates from the attempt to remove the questions from life. At its heart, it is fear-based.

Surrender

The fourth stage to redemptive community is surrender. Surrender does not come easy. This is one reason why the previous stage, chaos, is so pivotal. Chaos shows us that

---

[1] M. Scott Peck, *The Different Drum*, 90-91.

we cannot do it on our own, surrender opens the way for the one through whom redemptive community is possible; that is to say surrender is the bridge between our inability and God's ability. It is not until we have played our games (pseudocommunity), revealed our true nature (conflict), and poured forth our pitiful attempts (chaos), that we come to the end of ourselves. For the first time there is authenticity in the group. Through the act of surrender we are emptied of our agendas, our hang-ups, our rush to convert, heal, and fix each other.

Peck describes this stage (which he calls "emptiness") as:

> . . . a stage of hard, hard work, a time when the members work to empty themselves of everything that stands between them and community. And that is a lot. Many of the things that must be relinquished or sacrificed with integrity are virtual human universals: prejudices, snap judgments, fixed expectations, the desire to convert, heal, or fix, the urge to win, the fear of looking like a fool, the need to control. Other things may be exquisitely personal: hidden griefs, hatreds, or terrors that must be confessed, made public, before the individual can be fully "present" to the group. It is a time of risk and courage, and while it often feels relieving, it also often feels like dying.[1]

Surrender is the death that delivers the resurrection which is redemptive community. What is this death I speak of? It is the surrender of the will. The church rightly champions the redemptive death of Christ but is nearly mute (except of course in our theology) about the death we are called to which is the surrender of the will. Listen to the words of the modern mystic A. W. Tozer:

---

[1] M. Scott Peck, *A World Waiting to be Born*, 275.

We want to be saved but we insist that Christ do all the dying. No cross for us, no dethronement, no dying. We remain king within the little kingdom of Mansoul and wear our tinsel crown with all the pride of a Caesar; but we doom ourselves to shadows and weakness and spiritual sterility.[1]

I know of nothing else in the spiritual life we resist like the surrender of the will. We view this reality as the wild animal views the cage. We think it will be the end of us—and in one sense it will. But in this death we are born anew into our greater—our God-created Self. This is the way of the walk of life. C. S. Lewis describes this truth like this:

> Christ says "Give me All. I don't want so much of your time and so much of your money and so much of your work: I want you. I have not come to torment your natural self, but to kill it. . . . Hand over the whole natural self, all the desires you think innocent as well as the ones you think wicked—the whole outfit. I will give you a new self instead. In fact, I will give you Myself: my own will shall become yours."[2]

Upon first encounter, the stage of surrender (known for centuries in the church as *dying to the self-life*) may sound alluring because of the mysterious nature of the whole thing. If you do not already know, be warned, the surrender of the will is the hardest of all spiritual disciplines—and made harder by the fact that it is not a punctiliar, once-for-all act but rather one, for individuals and the collective group alike, we are called to again and again. I am convinced that it cannot be accomplished at all without the grace of God.

---

[1] A. W. Tozer, *The Root of the Righteous* (Christian Publications, Inc., 1955), 66.

[2] C. S. Lewis, *Mere Christianity*. (Macmillan Publishing Co., 1952) 167.

Redemptive Community

The group that perseveres will break into redemptive community. Actually, this wording is all wrong. It is not that we break into community but that community, like the dove of Christ, descends upon us, surrounding us and bathing us with a life that is wholly *other*. It is as if the whole affair has become a living sacrifice offered up, well-pleasing to God. There is joy, often hysterically so. There is awe and trembling. There is grief, there is sadness, there is happiness. In this time of *visitation*, to use the ancient expression, it is as though, perhaps for the first time, one experiences what it means to be a spiritual being, to be an integrated Self, to be fully alive.

A friend of mine described an experience he had in redemptive community on one occasion. It is the most beautiful expression of the phenomenon I have ever heard. My friend said "I was afraid to move. I was afraid I would bump into God."

If the church is going to battle its collective shadow as well as provide an environment where the solitary spiritual seeker can do likewise, if it is going to practice what it means to be the salt and light of the world, then there must be a return to redemptive community. Wayne Jacobsen is right, "The world is no longer impressed by our buildings and programs. They are looking for exactly what Jesus said they would—genuine love expressed between believers."[1]

---

[1] Wayne Jacobsen, *The Naked Church* (Harvest House Publishers, 1987), 185.

For the fact is that most of our human attempts to heal and convert prevent community. Human beings have within them a natural yearning and thrust toward health and wholeness and holiness. . . . Most of the time, however, this thrust, this energy is enchained by fear, neutralized by defenses and resistances. But put a human being in a truly safe place, where these defenses and resistances are no longer necessary, and the thrust toward health is liberated. When we are safe, there is a natural tendency for us to heal and convert ourselves. . . . Paradoxically, then, a group of humans becomes healing and converting only after its members have learned to stop trying to heal and convert.[1]

—M.Scott Peck

CHAPTER 9

Redemptive Community: A Return to Hope

At the outset let me say that without unnecessarily repeating them here, I claim the same caveats for myself and for churches in specific as I did in chapter five. Such a discussion as we are about to proceed with must, of necessity, speak in somewhat general terms and "paint with broad strokes," as it were.

It should be patently clear from the lengthy discussion of chapter five that the church should be a place where shadow work is undertaken as serious business. The begging question, then, is: "Does the church provide a forum where people are encouraged and equipped to engage their shadow, or has it become an environment which promotes shadowboxing?" By *shadowboxing* I do not mean to imply the notion of fighting a fictitious and imaginary opponent—for one can

---

[1] M. Scott Peck, *The Different Drum*, 68.

scarcely imagine a more real adversary than the shadow—but shadowboxing in the larger sense of *pretending* to fight? Sadly, it appears that the latter is true more often than not. John Sanford writes, "There is a darker side to our nature, . . . religion has so often pointed it out, *though even [in religion] there is a remarkable conspiracy within most of us to pay lip service to our darker nature, but avoid seeing it in the particular.*[1] (emphasis added)

Is Sanford correct? Is the church culpable of paying mere "lip service" to the shadow—of simply shadowboxing, if you will? Frequently, yes.

Let me illustrate. Susan and I have engaged in group therapy and group work for twenty years. Our experience, if not expertise, is significant. From experience, I can tell you that the following story is not at all unusual.

We were recently asked to conduct a group which would meet once weekly for two hours for a period of three months. The purpose of this group was to facilitate parent-child relationships and to give the parents insight in dealing with their children, all of whom were experiencing similar behavioral problems. As this was a church-related group, to my knowledge every participant in the group was a professing Christian.

Early in the group process Susan and I were sharing information with the parents regarding their own psychodynamic processes relative to their children and their children's problems. We were encountering very little involvement, some resistance, and a good bit of hostility by two (unrelated) members. Further, we could get no significant feedback from the group in terms of the material we were covering. The whole thing was becoming increasingly frustrating. We suspected we knew what the issue was. We had seen it many times before—but without feedback we could not be certain.

---

[1] John A. Sanford, *The Invisible Partners* (Paulist Press, 1980), 9-10.

A phone call from one of the participants, who had spoken to others in the group, validated our hunch. He called to say that he and his wife had sensed the frustration Susan and I were experiencing and that they just wanted to offer some encouragement. I assured him it was a timely call. "The problem," he said, "is that the material is too 'close to home.' We don't like seeing the truth about ourselves. We are not used to looking at ourselves to that degree."

There is an irony here. Again, this is not an atypical response from a Christian group. I have seen the same thing time and again while conducting various sorts of seminars and engaging in group work. The irony is, how can we yet be so unaccustomed to personal encounters with truth, with reality, in the church? I understand that truth can be painful. I feel the same way. But it has become almost alien! I understand that the shadow loathes it and flees from the truth. Mine does too. But there should be something within that, no matter how much the shadow protests, is drawn passionately to truth.

I appreciate the candid confession from my friend on the phone. However, for someone who has spent the last twenty-five years of his life in church (as he had) encounter with the truth was quite foreign and still something to be vehemently resisted. This was true also for many others in the group—at least for those he had spoken with.

I believe the church, quite unintentionally, is to blame for this mess in the thinking and understanding of its own. God help us. The product of the church today is all too often an immature, unconscious sort of saint that is not at all skilled in the practice of self-examination, conscious living, and the subsequent application of truth.

Why is this? There are two broad reasons. First, the church has lost sight of—in all but the most superficial of senses—the doctrine of the fall (Gen. 3). Second, the church has lost the concept of redemptive community and, therefore, has abandoned its practice. (Though certainly there is no shortage of "community groups" in our churches.) We will look extensively at this latter point. But first, some words about the fall.

Do We Really Believe In The Fall?

Recall the earlier words from Sanford. In the church, there is a remarkable conspiracy within most of us to pay lip service to our darker nature, while avoiding seeing it in the particular. If I had asked the group participants discussed above if they were sinners, I have not the slightest doubt that all would answer in the affirmative. But when given an opportunity to recognize and confront the specific aspects of their shadow, to be *specific sinners*, if I may coin a term, there were no takers. How could Susan and I possibly help this group of individuals confront their shadow and move toward wholeness if they were unwilling to recognize and own their shadow?

I truly believe that the church unwittingly fosters a sort of cognitive dissonance where the shadow is concerned. On the one hand sermons are preached, lessons are taught, and hymns are sung articulating the darkness abiding within the human personality. It is there in our creeds and statements of faith. We readily confess, "All have sinned, and fall short of the glory of God."

Curiously, however, when someone's darker side manifests itself, often the response is one of (at least feigned) utter amazement and complete incredulity—a behavior which would appear to invalidate the preaching, teaching, and singing which so utterly decry the human condition. It is as if the church is saying, "We are all fallen—but not really." Or perhaps, "We are all fallen—but our lives should never demonstrate this fact."

To the uninitiated secularist it must look as if the church is caught in the awkward and untenable position of strongly affirming the existence of the shadow while simultaneously being utterly shocked and nonplused when the shadow is encountered. In light of such curious evidence, one wonders how deep the understanding truly is in the church of the fact that we all have a dark side. It is as though the doctrine of the fall is really nothing more than an abstraction.

The matter is also confusing to initiates in the walk of life. Few people in the church talk and act like a combatant fighting the good fight. Winning some battles, losing others, encouraged by the knowledge that ultimately—our Lord's resurrection guarantees it—we will win the war. Rather, most of us act like (again, beyond our theological statements) there are no battles to fight, no shadow to engage. As I said, this creates a real dissonance in the mind of the new seeker. Fortunately, she has not learned to play the game. Unfortunately, she likely (if she stays in church) soon will.

I remember hearing a sermon when I was a young man, by a minister who was known to the world as a great spiritual leader. His subject was "Dealing With Failure." The famous man spoke of a time in his life when he felt he had really blown it. As a result of this flop, he was not sure if God could use him again. This failure occurred about thirty years in his life previous to the time I heard him deliver the sermon. This was the most encouraging address I ever heard as a young man. His subject had been something, as a relatively new traveler on the walk of life, I could relate to. I felt like I knew how to fail. His vulnerable admissions that night taught me that I was not the only one who struggled with failure. It also taught me that failure is not final.

New travelers to the walk of life need to hear this from others in the church, *especially* from those who have been on the road the longest. They need to hear that since

123

we are fallen, there are times that our life will show it—times when we will just flat screw-up. And they need to hear that failure need not be final.

Any counselor, therapist, or approachable pastor has likely heard a fellow believer say something like, "I am struggling with _____, but if word of this got to the church, I would be ruined."

To have a climate in the church which unwittingly fosters deception and dissociation is tragic and can lead to the observation that the church is not so much about encountering and overcoming the shadow as it is about denying that the shadow exists! To be sure, we are each responsible for our own behavior. Yet one wonders how many church leaders and other Christians could have been spared an ignominious fall if they had felt free to engage their shadow in a redemptive environment within the church. How can the church be a climate for individuation and growth (if true to its calling) if it is simultaneously reinforcing a duality in the human personality, a duality which arises from seeking to ignore or, worse, deny the existence of the shadow?

If there really was a fall, then we are all fallen. The saint is not one in whom there is an absence of shadow but rather one in whom there is the presence of spiritual warfare. Otherwise, what is grace for?

Redemptive Community— The Way To Wholeness

A wise and valuable Buddhist teaching is that, "Without a Sangha [community], you will be lost."[1] I mentioned earlier that the church should be a place where individuals are free and equipped to engage their shadow in a redemp-

---

[1] Thich Nhat Hanh, *Living Buddha, Living Christ* (Riverhead Books, 1995), 68.

tive environment. This is not a light matter. In fact, this is precisely the purpose of the church. *As its core purpose, the church is called to redemptive community.* We are called both to *be* a redemptive community and we are called to the *practice* of redemptive community.[1]

These two terms *redemption* and *community* beg definition. The most common Biblical usage of the term redemption means the payment of a ransom. Another word commonly translated redemption in the New Testament refers to the act of purchasing in the local market place. Interestingly, most often the market referred to by the usage of this word is the first-century slave market.

In claiming for himself the title Redeemer and in saying that he came in order that he might redeem, Christ is identifying himself as the one who paid the ransom price that we might be freed from enslavement to the shadow life.

When I speak of the church *as a* community I have in mind the idea of, what I call, "redemptive interrelatedness." Dietrich Bonhoeffer is exactly right when he says, "Christianity means community through Jesus Christ and in Jesus Christ. No Christian community is more or less than this."[2]

Out of this reality, the reality of the church *as a* community based on redemptive interrelatedness, should come the *practice of* community. (In this respect, the matter is similar to the idea of the fall discussed previously. There is no benefit to the church saying we *are* a redemptive community if she is embracing this fact only as an abstraction without *practicing* redemptive community.) Community is the living out of our redemptive interrelatedness. The former point is a theological fact. Christ has established the church

---

[1] The subject of redemptive community is at once so large and so important that it is a book unto itself. Here, we can do little more than introduce the subject and consider some of its more salient characteristics.

[2] Dietrich Bonhoeffer, *Life Together* (Harper & Row, 1954), 21.

as a redemptive community. But this fact is of very little practical consequence to the church or to the world unless the body of Christ is actively engaging in the practice of redemptive community. In theological terminology, the church *as a* redemptive community is orthodoxy; the church *practicing* redemptive community is orthopraxis.[1] Today, the praxis of redemptive community is virtually nonexistent.

As praxis, what does redemptive community look like? What are its dynamics, its components? What are the salient features we can look for when belief and behavior merge? Fortunately, we have a book, the New Testament, chock-full of insights to this question. Further, we have the wisdom of others who have labored long and hard in the study of redemptive community.

Restoration - The Purpose of Redemptive Community

Redemptive community is symbiotically related to the doctrine of the fall. By his redemptive work on the cross, Christ has effectually freed us from the curse of the fall (see Romans 5). Although the work will not be finalized in us until his return to reign, the ransom payment has nevertheless been made and the work is underway.

The high calling of the church is to provide a context in which those who have committed to their spiritual life and development can share in community with others on the walk of life. It is a call to nothing short of reclaiming for ourselves all that was lost in the fall. This is why I prefer the term *redemptive* community. And it is the only way for the church to effectively confront its own shadow.

Redemption implies restoration. It is through the practice of redemptive community that God commences the

---

[1] Praxis is the outworking, the practice of a theory or principle; it is where belief and behavior merge.

process of restoring to himself, and to us, all that was lost in the fall. We begin to recapture, little by little, the knowledge and experience shared by the archetypal couple as they walked with God and with each other in the garden. In redemptive community we reclaim for ourselves incrementally what it is to know and live with God aright, and what it is to know and live with ourselves and others aright.

To Israel in exile God promised "I will restore you to health and heal your wounds."[1] This is what we seek in redemptive community. But there is more. In another place we read, "They will rebuild the ancient ruins and restore the places long devastated; they will renew the ruined cities that have been devastated for generations."[2] Do you see it? The pronouns have changed. In the first passage God says *I* will do this. In the second, he says *they* (i.e., the people) will do this. We are co-laborers with God in the restorative work of redemptive community. As the church does the hard work of community he will meet with us and do his part.

Restoration is growth. It is psychospiritual development. Restoration, through the practice of redemptive community, is the way in which not only our individual shadows but the collective shadow of the church as well is confronted and integrated in a healthy, nondestructive way.

Further, restoration is a process. I believe the church has skewed this reality. By emphasizing the punctiliar "decision," great harm has been done. Many have been coerced into "making a decision for Christ" against the preparedness of their own spiritual state at the time. As a result, not a few of these people have been turned off, sometimes for good, to spiritual realities. Listen to these honest and brave words spoken by a renowned pastor:

---

[1] Jer. 30:17.

[2] Isa. 61:4.

It has always seemed unfair to me that many churches (and some individual Christians) keep careful records on how many converts they make to Christianity, but never keep any records at all on how many they drive away from Christ. Fairness would seem to dictate that both sides of the ledger should be maintained. For the fact is, churches often turn far more people from Christ than they ever win to him, and frequently it is the most zealous and orthodox of Christians who are doing the driving away.[1]

We engage in the work of redemptive community in anticipation of that day when God restores all things to their rightful place, just as he has promised.[2] Until that time our prayer should be that of the psalmist, "Restore us, O God; make your face shine upon us, that we may be delivered."

Love - The Context of Redemptive Community

Wayne Jacobsen gives us an excellent summation of redemptive community when he says "Community . . . is God loving people through each other as they respond to the uniqueness of the moment and the moving of the Holy Spirit."[3] In community, we are conduits of God's redemptive love. We are channels through which God demonstrates the importance of each member and through which he brings the message of the hour that our soul needs.

This is precisely why a church consumed by its own shadow is so devastating to those in it and around it. There is no divine love pouring through such a church. Think back to the earlier information on the shadow of the church. Think of the discussion on divorce. When the church operates out

---

[1] Ray C. Stedman, *Authentic Christianity* (Multnomah Press, 1975), 15.

[2] Acts 3:21.

[3] Wayne Jacobsen, *The Naked Church*, 183.

of its shadow on this subject no love flows to these already devastated individuals. They feel as though they are lepers—castaways. This is the very antitheses of divine love. "We will love you as long as we approve of you," is the message the church sends when it behaves this way. At this point, the church becomes irrelevant. The world reeks of this message already.

The greater essence of love is not an emotion but a volition—it is an act of the will. (The act of will through which love must first show itself in community is that of commitment.) If we do not recognize this we will end up loving only those we like. That is, we will love only those we are drawn to by our emotions. Again, the church is not needed if this is the message it intends to send. Society already serves up this type of love regularly.

C. S. Lewis puts it well:

> The rule for all of us is perfectly simple. Do not waste time bothering whether you "love" your neighbor; act as if you did. As soon as we do this we find one of the great secrets. When you are behaving as if you loved someone, you will presently come to love him. If you injure someone you dislike, you will find yourself disliking him more. If you do him a good turn, you will find yourself disliking him less. There is, indeed, one exception. If you do him a good turn, not to please God and obey the law of [love], but to show him what a fine forgiving chap you are, and to put him in your debt, and then sit down to wait for his "gratitude," you will probably be disappointed. (People are not fools: they have a very quick eye for anything like showing off, or patronage.) But whenever we do good to another self, just because it is another self, made (like us) by God, and desiring its own happiness as we desire ours, we shall have learned to love it a little more or, at least, to dislike it less.[1]

---

[1] C. S. Lewis, *Mere Christianity*, 116.

We are to love with that love which God craves to pour into our hearts by his Spirit. This is the love which forms the context of redemptive community. Nothing else will do.

Inclusion - The Attitude of Redemptive Community

Earlier we looked at Romans 12, where we are encourage not to allow the culture around us to squeeze us into its own mold. Were Paul to write this today I believe he would add, "Oh yes—and don't let the church squeeze you into its own mold either!" Fear of difference is a massive component in the church's shadow. Both consciously and unconsciously pressure is applied to spiritual seekers to conform, to get in line.

This behavior always stifles life. Community is never achieved by coercion. The motto of redemptive community is *unity through diversity*. More often it appears that the motto of the church is *uniformity through constraint*. This has always been a problem.

"Welcome with open arms fellow believers who don't see things the way you do," Paul writes in Romans 14. He adds:

> And don't jump all over them every time they do or say something you don't agree with—even when it seems that they are strong on opinions but weak in the faith department. Remember, they have their own history to deal with. Treat them gently.

When we fail to accept one another it is because we have taken upon ourselves the role of judge (and not seldom, of jury as well!). This is not our department. Further, we will kill redemptive community as long as we persist in behaving this way. Redemptive community is about inclusion and acceptance, not exclusion.

Again, the church has had this sort of behavior in its shadow from the very outset. Paul continues:

> Do you have any business crossing people off the guest list or interfering with God's welcome? If there are corrections to be made or manners to be learned, God can handle that without your help. . . .
>
> That's why Jesus lived and died and then lived again: so that he could be our Master across the entire range of life and death, and free us from the petty tyrannies of each other.
>
> So where does that leave you when you criticize a brother? And where does that leave you when you condescend to a sister? I'd say it leaves you looking pretty silly—or worse. . . . So tend to your knitting. You've got your hands full just taking care of your own life before God.

Redemptive community does not abolish the person by attempting to coerce her into fitting some arbitrary notion of how she should be. This only serves to stifle the individual and to hamper the work of God in and through her. Uniformity is why numerous people have left the church, after having found it to be so bloody dull and constricting.

The walk of life is not like an interstate. It is more like a country trail that begins at our own door and winds its way through the woods, over the rolling hills and rocky crags, across the streams and rivers, and through the thickets and marshes until at long last we reach trail's end. Redemptive community does not forever shout at everyone else on the journey that they must abandon the path that begins at their door and join us, forsaking their path for our own. Instead, it recognizes that we each have our own path to take on the walk of life and that ultimately, we all arrive at the same destination in Christ.

Remember, "Jesus lived and died and then lived again: so that he could be our Master across the entire range of life and death, and free us from the petty tyrannies of each other."[1]

A final word about inclusion as the attitude of redemptive community. Inclusion is not to be confused with tolerance. While inclusive acceptance includes tolerance, it is much more. I can tolerate you without ever embracing you. But this is not the way of redemptive community. True inclusion incorporates the individual into the community.

Edification - The Work of the Redemptive Community

Edification is an intriguing concept. The basic word, "edify," (oikodome) was used by the ancient Greeks to speak of building a house. Paul uses the term in his letters to the various churches to describe how we are to build one another up in faith. Edification is nothing less than working to promote the spiritual development of each member as we participate in redemptive community.

The edification we are called to practice is a *mutual* edification. No one is left out. The edification that redemptive community promotes extends to the lowliest and least powerful member of the group and in point of fact, makes no such false distinctions between its members.

What does edification consist of? It all depends. There are many tools to be used in the process of edifying one another. Further, we each need to be edified in different ways at different times in our lives.

Confrontation is sometimes called for in the process of edification. Recall earlier I mentioned how Paul confronted Peter "to his face" because of certain behaviors in Peter which were creating confusion and causing dissension in the church.

---

[1] Rom. 14:9, *THE MESSAGE.*

Was this an act of edification on Paul's behalf? Absolutely. Peter's behavior was shutting down the experience of community. He needed to be confronted. Paul's act not only edified the group but Peter as well. This confrontation contributed to Peter's spiritual development.

Teaching, that is, instruction in living, edifies the church, as does preaching—or so it should. There are few things more irritating than listening to a sermon that seems to be proceeding from an angry heart or a heart poisoned with bitterness. They certainly do not edify. We need instruction. We need to have our understanding enlarged. In this respect the church should function as a kind of spiritual academy. It is for this very reason that God has provide to the church women and men who are skilled teachers, gifted by him to impart spiritual realities.

Correction edifies. From time to time we all need correcting. Our shadow can blind us. In the practice of redemptive community others are there to say to us "you're wrong about this," or "you need to address this behavior, this attitude you have." God uses this feedback, if we will allow him, to take us further down the road. A word of warning to pastors here. I have seen many pastors who felt they were beyond the corrective input of those in their church. They were insulted, even outraged by it. This is a poisonous attitude that sooner or later will kill the spirit of community.

There is another type of edification that is similar to correction but differs in the matter of degree. It is much stronger than correction. I am speaking of the *rebuke*. Rebuking takes a lot of grace—for both the giver and the receiver. But, administered and received properly, it is an instrument of edification. To this day, I can recall a rebuke I received some 18 years ago as though it were only yesterday. I can remember every detail, even down to where the giver of the rebuke and I were both standing at the time. It was well deserved. I was both a young pastor (then 24) and a high school history teacher at the time. It was Monday morning and I had just stepped into the classroom of a fellow teacher to chat before classes began. I had spoken to a group of married couples at her church the Saturday previous and she was expressing to me how she and her husband had benefitted from the material I shared. Giving her the line I had heard so many times and had ignorantly and thoughtlessly adopted I said, "Well, thank you but, you know, it really wasn't me. It was the Lord."

Man, did she let me have it. "You pastors," she said. "Why do you say something stupid like that every time someone tries to show you appreciation. Do you think I don't know God gets the ultimate glory. I wasn't worshiping you. I was just saying thanks for your ministry to us!" It was as if I had opened the door to a blast furnace! After I had combed my hair and put the fire out I said "You're right. That was utter crap. Thank you for that." I'm not usually that defenseless but it was as if God gave me the grace to stand the blast of that powerful rebuke. It was a good rebuke. My statement to her had been complete bull and was nothing more than a stupid, arrogant (thinly disguised as humble, of course) cliché. I've never used it again.

Encouragement is another instrument of edification. When we encourage someone we "prop them up on the leaning side," as a mentor of mine use to say. The problem with life is that it is so daily. There is no one on the walk of life who does not grow weary from time to time. How good it is when an encourager comes along to build us up. Late into my years as a pastor two men came into our church and into my life who took it upon themselves to become my encouragers. They were a golden gift to me. They were as cool water to a parched throat. Thank you, Gary. Thank you, Donnie.

The last tool of edification we shall consider (although there are many more) is really a couplet. I am talking about *forgiveness* and *restoration*. The church is the only army on record that routinely shoots its wounded. It has been rightly noted that, "We do more damage to ourselves than we have ever done to the gates of hell. Honest confession of sin is lost because such confession is usually used to judge rather than to forgive and cleanse."[1] When the church functions like this, it has ceased to be a redemptive community. And the watching world knows it.

Interdependence - The Framework of Redemptive Community

There are no superfluous parts to the Body of Christ. In redemptive community everyone is important and everyone is of equal importance. Using the human body as a metaphor the Apostle Paul describes this interdependence to the church at Corinth:

> Now the body is not made up of one part but of many. If the foot should say, "Because I am not a hand, I do not belong to the body," it would not for that reason cease to be part of the body. And if the ear should say, "Because I am not an eye, I do not belong to the body," it would not for that reason cease to be part of the body. If the whole body were an eye, where would the sense of hearing be? If the whole body were an ear, where would the sense of smell be? But in fact God has arranged the parts in the body, every one of them, just as he wanted them to be. If they were all one part, where would the body be? As it is, there are many parts, but one body.[2]

America has come to represent individualism gone mad—and so to, I am afraid, has the American church. We

[1] Wayne Jacobsen, *The Naked Church*, 184.

[2] 1 Cor. 12:14-20.

have lost the understanding of our interdependence upon one another.[1] Consequently, those in the church who have attained celebrity status (on whatever level) entertain while the vast majority of the church sits and watches. Both parties are equally guilty. The celebrities get their egocentric egos stroked while the "audience" gets spared from any real involvement. This is not community.

This interdependent aspect of redemptive community is described for us in the following words:

> You're [those who have commenced the walk of life] no longer wandering exiles. This kingdom of faith is now your home country. You're no longer strangers or outsiders. You *belong* here, with as much right to the name Christian as anyone. God is building a home. He's using us all—irrespective of how we got here—in what he is building. He used the apostles and prophets for the foundation. Now he's using you, fitting you in brick by brick, stone by stone, with Christ Jesus as the cornerstone that holds all the parts together. We see it taking shape day after day—a holy temple built by God, all of us built into it, a temple in which God is quite at home.[2]

As I pointed out in chapter five, there is equality in the redemptive community. Hierarchies based on racial and ethnic distinctions are abolished, class hierarchies are abolished, and so are those based on gender. If the church is ever to eradicate these biases from its shadow, it will do so only by embracing the interdependence that redemptive community brings.

---

[1] We are called to all three: independence, dependence, and interdependence. The imbalance today swings toward an overemphasis of independence.

[2] Eph. 2:19-22.

Confession & Prayer - The Sacraments of Redemptive Community

I must warn you. The words you are about to read are a trap! The Apostle James writes, "Make this your common practice: Confess your sins to each other and pray for each other so that you can live together whole and healed. The prayer of a person living right with God is something powerful to be reckoned with."

Does that not sound beautiful? We all want to be whole. We all want to be healed deep within our souls. We all want to know the kind of power that comes from a life of spiritual integrity. What an alluring prospect. But I know of no discipline to the spiritual life that is harder to practice than confession. And I have heard many others admit the same thing. So hard is this in fact, that most people simply don't do it—and I am referring to those who are *on* the walk of life! There is no redemptive community without this, however.

Public confession was a routine practice of the early church. This was not done in some rote group fashion as (if at all) it is today. Rather, an individual would stand up in the congregation and confess publically to particular, specific acts of commission and omission. With the legitimization of Christianity under Constantine (early fourth century), the practice of personal public confession eventually ceased and was replaced with private confession before a priest, replete with guaranteed confidentiality. The argument can be made that the cessation of the practice of public confession marked the end of real community in the church.

Personal confession is hard, I suspect, because it is so valuable. Satan knows this—and so does the shadow. Most of us will gladly confess our sins to God. That seems safe enough (most of the time!). But this is not the confession James is speaking of. Confess *to one another*, James says.

No one has spoken more eloquently to this issue than Dietrich Bonhoeffer. He shines a searing light on one of the darkest and deepest aspects of the church's shadow. I quote him at length here:

> He who is alone with his sin is utterly alone. It may be that Christians, notwithstanding corporate worship, common prayer, and all their fellowship in service, may still be left to their loneliness. The final breakthrough to fellowship does not occur, because, though they have fellowship with one another as believers and as devout people, they do not have fellowship as the undevout, as sinners. So everybody must conceal his sin from himself and from the fellowship. We dare not be sinners. Many Christians are unthinkably horrified when a real sinner is suddenly discovered among the righteous. So we remain alone with our sin, living in lies and hypocrisy. The fact is that we *are* sinners!
>
> . . . In confession the break-through to community takes place. Sin demands to have a man by himself. It withdraws him from the community. The more isolated a person is, the more destructive will be the power of sin over him, and the more deeply he becomes involved in it, the more disastrous is his isolation. Sin wants to remain unknown. It shuns the light. In the darkness of the unexpressed it poisons the whole being of a person. This can happen even in the midst of a pious community. In confession the light of the Gospel breaks into the darkness and seclusion of the heart. The sin must be brought into the light. The unexpressed must be openly spoken and acknowledged. All that is secret and hidden is made manifest. It is a hard struggle until the sin is openly admitted. But God breaks gates of brass and bars of iron (Ps. 107:16).[1]

---

[1] Dietrich Bonhoeffer, *Life Together*, 110, 112.

Do you see why interpersonal confession is so important? It breaks the power of the shadow. It recognizes the fact that we are as sick as our secrets. I have no doubt this is why both great enemies of the spiritual life, Satan and the shadow, fight it with such vigor.

In the Vietnam war there was a gutsy soldier known as the *tunnel rat.* This was a job with few takers. The job of a tunnel rat was to crawl through the myriad labyrinthine tunnels that ran like veins under the earth of South Vietnam and ferret out the enemy. (One captured Viet Cong said that he traveled 200 miles from North Vietnam to Saigon—all underground!) This is what our psyche develops into when we fail to practice confession. We are alone, crawling about in the darkness of our own soul, just as Bonhoeffer says. We get lost within. The farther we go the darker, the more dangerous it gets. Confession, as painful as it is, brings my psyche to the light. It delivers me from the chaos of my darkness where both sight and safety are at risk. It keeps me from losing my own soul, even while I am in the midst of the church.

The second great sacrament of redemptive community, along with interpersonal confession, is that of prayer. James is not talking about prayer in general. The context of this passage clearly indicates that he is talking about a special *kind* of prayer. He is referring to prayer that is to accompany confession. As we confess our sins, the redemptive community we are involved in prays for us—prays that God would heal us from the ravages of sin and shadow and that he would make us whole. (Interestingly, *heal* and *health, whole,* and *holy* all come from the same root word.) This is the sacramental prayer that is concomitant with confession in the redemptive community. This is the combination that unleashes vibrant spiritual power.

Freedom - The Consequence of Redemptive Community

The practice of redemptive community is liberating. Earlier I referred to the prayer in Psalm 80:3, "Restore us, O God; make your face shine upon us, that we may be delivered." Another excellent translation for the last phrase of that prayer is ". . . that we may be set free." This is what happens when God's face shines upon us in redemptive community. The result is freedom.[1]

I believe that essentially there are four restraints to psychospiritual development God liberates us from as we practice redemptive community: our egocentric self, our personal hindrances to psychospiritual development, our illusions, and unconscious living.

Regarding enslavement to the egocentric lifestyle Wayne Jacobsen writes, "We have confused independence with freedom. To live by our own desires, to ignore the input of others, to care only about our own needs—these are the tools of darkness."

We all come into this world with an egocentric view of the universe. That is, we are born thinking the world revolves around us. We are natural born narcissists and, like the young man I mentioned in chapter one who could not believe that the girl in the sandwich shop had forgotten (from the previous week!) how he wanted his sandwich, most people never seem to grow out of their egocentric view of the world. It is my opinion that this is the greatest deliverance God gives us—deliverance from our egocentric self. In redemptive community God will drive this narcissistic bondage from us and set us free. In fact, this is one reason why, at the onset, community can result in such conflict.

---

[1] If the reader would like to do a revealing study, trace the concept of freedom through Paul's writings. The word is pivotal in Pauline theology and to the spiritual life in general.

Imagine a room full of people simultaneously, yet individually and personally, learning that they are not the center of the universe! The god *Ego* does not die without a fight.

We are told by the author of Hebrews to "throw off everything that hinders and the sin that so easily entangles" us. Excellent advise—hard to do. We each have our own hindrances to the spiritual life. Mine are not yours perhaps, and yours are not mine. Our shadows differ, and so do our hindrances. What we do share in common however is "the sin that so easily entangles us." This allusion is exegetically tricky. I believe, in keeping with the warning he has given throughout the book, the speaker is talking about the ever-present temptation to chunk it all, give up the fight, and abandon the walk of life. Elsewhere he has warned us that the tougher times get, the more we need to practice redemptive community. Why? The answer is quite obvious. The tougher the times, the greater the temptation to bail out. The practice of true community can liberate us from "everything that hinders" us as we pursue the walk of life. And it can safeguard us from the "sin that so easily entangles," which, again, is nothing less than the temptation to scrap it all and walk away.

But redemptive community is not only concerned with preventing the abandonment of the walk of life, it is also earnestly concerned with those who have already done so. Listen to the Apostle James: "My dear friends, if you know people who have wandered off from God's truth, don't write them off. Go after them. Get them back and you will have rescued precious lives from destruction and prevented an epidemic of wandering away from God."[1]

Redemptive community has the power to free us from our illusions. Before discussing this perhaps it would be useful to say a word about these psychological mechanisms. Illu-

---

[1] James 5:19-20, *THE MESSAGE.*

sions are wish-based beliefs. They are the temptation to view things as one desires them to be, rather than as they actually are. Consequently, the unconscious purpose of an illusion is to construct a view of some given facet of life which is more palatable than reality itself. Freud taught us that the strength of an illusion is determined by the strength of the wish behind it. That is to say, the stronger the wish—the stronger the illusion. In short, an illusion is a psychological adaptation one employs to help him face life.

In community, our illusions are checked by the other members of the group. Redemptive community is ever calling us to a reality-oriented approach to life. Listen once again to Bonhoeffer:

> By sheer grace, God will not permit us to live even for a brief period in a dream world. . . . Only that fellowship which faces such disillusionment, with all its unhappy and ugly aspects, begins to be what it should be in God's sight, begins to grasp in faith the promise that is given to it. The sooner this shock of disillusionment comes to an individual and to a community the better for both. A community which cannot bear and cannot survive such a crisis, which insists upon keeping its illusion when it should be shattered, permanently loses in that moment the promise of Christian community. Sooner or later it will collapse. Every human wish dream that is injected into the Christian community is a hindrance to genuine community and must be banished if genuine community is to survive. He who loves his dream of a community more than the Christian community itself becomes a destroyer of the latter, even though his personal intentions may be ever so honest and earnest and sacrificial.[1]

As I said earlier, redemptive community provides a reality check. "You shall know the truth," our Lord said, "and the truth will set you free."

---

[1] Dietrich Bonhoeffer, *Life Together*, 27.

The final freedom which we will discuss (there are surely more) that emanates from redemptive community is liberation from unconscious living. Unconsciousness is a pervasive enemy of spiritual development. As we engage with our fellow pilgrims in community, truth and insight is brought to our consciousness. We see things about ourselves, both as individuals and as a community, that we were completely oblivious to. The subject of unconsciousness is of such importance that we will be discussing it at length in chapter ten.

Celebration - The Joy of Redemptive Community

I know for a fact that going to church can potentially be a dull experience. Redemptive community, however, is not. I do not mean for a moment to imply that the practice of community is always a hoot. Sometimes it's a drag. It is painful to examine yourself, to confess to one another, to be corrected, rebuked, and the like. But what incredible celebration awaits those who persevere and participate in redemptive community. There is nothing in all the world like it—literally!

Listen to the exuberance with which Paul discusses the celebration to be found in redemptive community:

So reach out and welcome one another to God's glory. Jesus did it; now *you* do it! . . . Just think of all the Scriptures that will come true in what we do! For instance:

"Then I'll join outsiders in a hymn-sing;
I'll sing to your name!"

And this one:

"Outsiders and insiders, rejoice together!"

And again:

"People of all nations, celebrate God!
All colors and races, give hearty praise!"

... Oh! May the God of green hope fill you up with joy, fill
you up with peace, so that your believing lives, filled with
the life-giving energy of the Holy Spirit, will brim over with
hope![1]

The celebration we experience in redemptive community is a tune-up really. We are in training, as the Spirit
of joy prepares us for what the final book of the Bible calls
the "Wedding Supper of the Lamb."[2]

Epiphany - The Mystery of Redemptive Community

Epiphany is the sudden perception or manifestation
of the essential nature of a thing. Redemptive community is
mysterious in its very nature—in its essential nature. It is
supernatural and herein lies its mystery.

I must confess, I have been preoccupied with getting
to this point since the very beginning of this chapter. What
is to be said here is of such importance that it has been on
my conscious mind as I put to paper all that has gone before.

What I have longed to tell you is this, and it is imperative that you understand, just as I must. Redemptive
community cannot really be dissected, as I have attempted
to do for you up to this point. The sum is infinitely greater
than its parts. There is a mystery that sweeps over and
through true community as God's Spirit breathes life into
the very process. I, thank God, cannot explain it; but I have
experienced it on numerous occasions. I am just thankful
that we can know experientially what our reason cannot
comprehend or quantify.

The spiritual seeker is not unfamiliar with mystery.
Our Lord described his very kingdom as a mystery. Redemp-

---

[1] Rom. 15:7-13, *THE MESSAGE*.

[2] Rev. 19:9, *THE MESSAGE*.

tive entry into that kingdom is called a mystery. Spiritual truth is considered mysterious to the natural mind, as is the return of Christ. The church as the body of Christ is a mystery, and so is the truth of the indwelling Christ. Indeed, the very prospect of the spiritual life is itself a mystery.[1]

So we are not distressed by the mystery which surrounds redemptive community. We merely raise our hearts in celebration and marvel at it all.

If Jung is correct and confronting the shadow is the first stage down the path of psychospiritual growth, then it is incumbent upon the church, as well as each of us as individuals, to consider the matter of the shadow. Furthermore, if Jung is right, this is serious medicine for the church. If stage one to individuation (wholeness) is confrontation of the shadow, and the church unwittingly fosters a climate resistant to this, what this says about the actual spirituality of the church is not terribly flattering.

The church should be a place where the light of grace can illumine our shadow, imparting the courage and strength necessary to confront the shadow in a redemptive context, to the end result of personal and corporate growth. When the church becomes just such an environment, perhaps Jung will be proven right in his statement that to complete the education of the soul, to move ever closer to the ultimate goal of individuation, people may have to go back to the church when they reach a certain stage of analysis.[2]

---

[1] Should the reader like to examine the biblical references to the points I have mentioned here, they are, in the order I referred to them: Mt. 13:11, Rom. 16:25, 1 Cor. 4:1, 1 Cor. 15:51, Eph. 3 and 5:32, Col. 1:27, and 1 Tim. 3:16.

[2] C. G. Jung, *C. G. Jung Speaking* (Princeton University Press, 1977), 440. As an illustration of this very point, one Jungian analyst remarks, "I left the church because it was dead and boring. Now I go back and appreciate services in a way I never could before." Erica Goode, "Spiritual Questing," 68.

Part Five:

THE WALK OF LIFE

*And I said to the man who stood at the gate of the year:
'Give me a light that I may tread safely into the unknown.' And he replied: 'Go out into the darkness and
put your hand into the hand of God. That shall be to
you better than light and safer than a known way.'*[1]

—M. Louise Haskins

CHAPTER 10

Out of the Darkness

One of the more salient metaphors used to describe
the pursuit of psychospiritual growth is that of a pilgrimage—a journey. (Among the earliest ancient pilgrims was
the patriarch Abraham.) The idea was popularized many
centuries later in Bunyan's classic *The Pilgrim's Progress*. Personally, I call this journey, this pilgrimage toward
psychospiritual growth, *the walk of life*. Let me say I am quite
convinced about all of this. I believe our psychospiritual
growth is *the*, not *a* walk of life.

If there is a more seminal task than striving to claim all
that we are heirs to spiritually—our rightful inheritance, if you
will—and to help others do likewise through the practice of
redemptive community, honestly I cannot fathom what that
would be. We all have different vocational callings but we are
all partakers of the same psychospiritual calling. This is the call
to the walk of life.

It has been said that anyone over thirty-five for whom
death is not the main preoccupation is a fool. I see the point
but I think the primary noun is wrong. If *life* were our fore-

---

[1] M. Louise Haskins, as quoted by King George VI of England in his Christ-
mas radio broadcast, 25 December 1939.

most consideration, then our death would pretty much iron out its own problems.

The walk of life, like any other journey, has a point of departure and a destination. It is a walk out of and away from something and a walk into and toward something. To put it succinctly, the walk of life is the walk out of the darkness (shadow) and into the light—out of unconsciousness and into consciousness. In therapy, I often illustrate this with reference to an iceberg. Only ten percent of an iceberg is above the water line while ninety percent of the mammoth chunk of ice lies hidden below, buried beneath the ocean surface. This is like the consciousness/unconsciousness issue. In fact, research indicates that consciousness occupies only twelve percent of the mind. The overwhelming majority of people live the bulk of their lives operating out of unconsciousness rather than consciousness. The challenge of life is to work toward ever-increasing percentages in favor of conscious living.

As its point of departure the walk of life is out of and away from the darkness of the unconscious, shadowy approach to life. This is the beginning of the journey toward psychospiritual wholeness. In this chapter we will be looking first at the unconscious life and then, lastly, at what it means to confront the shadow.

The Unconscious Life

Recall our beginnings, back in part one. I spoke of spiritual darkness and the dystopic consequences of that darkness upon ourselves and society at large. The darkness which we must strive to eradicate in our lives is that of unconscious living. Unconsciousness is the life's blood of the shadow.

Many times in therapy I have seen consciousness break upon a person. It is like a great veil has been lifted in their mind and they suddenly and for the first time see the truth about a particular thing. "I had no idea," "I never dreamed this was the case," "I can't believe I couldn't see this," are the types of statements expressed at those times. The person is utterly amazed that he could be in such darkness, completely nonplused that he had not seen this before.

Perhaps I should explain something of extreme importance about unconscious living. Unconscious means *not known*. It does not mean *unknowable*. This is precisely why unconscious living cannot be lightly excused. We do not have to live this way. (As I have remarked elsewhere, Freud tells us that the purpose of psychotherapy is to make the unconscious conscious.)

Not all unconscious living emanates from a malicious heart. Laziness and lack of vigilance required for psychospiritual growth is often the culprit. The pursuit of growth requires energy, it requires deliberate effort. Many of the ills of society, not to mention our own psychospiritual attrition, are due not to any deliberate vicious intent but simply to lazy living.

Back again to the iceberg. The more our life lies below the water line in the cold, the dark, the unconscious, the less growth we experience. The great danger of unconscious living lies in the very fact that it is unconscious. Psychospiritual darkness is thus self-perpetuating. Ironically, one of the clearest examples of unconscious living available to us is the life of the Apostle Paul. Just as he would later model for us what it is to pursue spiritual growth and to do battle with the shadow, in his early adult years he was a prime example of abject unconscious living.

As a young man Paul (then known by his birth name of Saul) was one of those people who is among the most dangerous and destructive human beings ever to walk the earth. He was a religious zealot. He hunted down the first generation Christians like a wild animal, seeking their imprisonment and even death. In fact, Saul was present at the death of the first Christian martyr, Stephen, who was murdered by stoning (being pelted with rocks). Listen to the record: "As the rocks rained down, Stephen prayed, 'Master Jesus, take my life.' Then he knelt down, praying loud enough for everyone to hear, 'Master, don't blame them for this sin'—his last words. Then he died. Saul was right there, congratulating the killers."[1] So blinded was Saul by his own unconsciousness that he actually thought this murder had been a good deed. He gave praise to the killers, congratulating them for a job well done!

The story goes on. His blind zealotry stirred to even greater heights by Stephen's death, Saul redoubles his efforts to wipe out the young church:

> [The stoning of Stephen] set off a terrific persecution of the church in Jerusalem. The believers were all scattered throughout Judea and Samaria. . . .
>
> And Saul just went wild, devastating the church, entering house after house, dragging men and women off to jail.[2]

The only thing that rescued Paul was the spiritual birth that placed him on the walk of life. Until that point, he was the quintessential example of the fact that one can be drenched in religion without being alive spiritually.

And he would have no doubt continued in his unconscious blindness had God not intervened in his life. On a day like many others before Saul awoke and went in search of believers to persecute. He was "breathing out murderous threats against them," the record tells us. On this particular day he went to the high priest to get arrest warrants so that if he should find any followers of Christ in the synagogues of Damascus he could arrest them—man or woman—and bring them to Jerusalem to stand trial. While on the road to

---

[1] Acts 7:59-60, *THE MESSAGE.*
[2] Acts 8:1-3, *THE MESSAGE.*

Damascus, Saul had an experience which would alter his life forever. This is his autobiographical account of the event:

> About noon as I came near Damascus, suddenly a bright light from heaven flashed around me. I fell to the ground and heard a voice say to me, "Saul! Saul! Why do you persecute me?"
>
> "Who are you, Lord?" I asked.
>
> "I am Jesus of Nazareth, whom you are persecuting," he replied. My companions saw the light, but they did not understand the voice of him who was speaking to me.
>
> "What shall I do, Lord?" I asked.
>
> "Get up," the Lord said, "and go into Damascus. There you will be told all that you have been assigned to do." My companions led me by the hand into Damascus, because the brilliance of the light had blinded me.[1]

It was this spiritual encounter with Christ which delivered Saul from his unconsciousness. He was blinded temporarily that he might come to see forever. He who was the fiercest persecutor of the early believers was now led by the hand like a baby to the very people whom he had been persecuting. Why? So that he might receive instruction from those wise in the life of the spirit and thus be brought into greater consciousness—and so that he might learn of the walk of life.

The account of the early life of Paul (Saul) brings to light a fact that is as scary as it is important: *Most of the destruction unleashed in the world is done so by people who "know"—beyond a shadow of a doubt—that they are absolutely doing the right thing.* Think of Hitler and his hacks in the Third Reich. Think of Idi Amin, Uganda's deposed dictator. Think of his maniacal Cambodian counterpart, Pol Pot. Like

---

[1] Acts 22:6-11.

the young Saul, these people and all like them are never troubled by the prospect that maybe, just maybe, they could be wrong. This is the unconscious approach to life.

But unconsciousness works its havoc in thousands of lives every day that differs from the examples above only in matters of degree of influence and extent of the damage done. There is the boss who creates a stifling attitude at work because of her "It's my way or the highway" approach. There is the unteachable parent who will not so much as entertain the idea that he might blow it on occasion and who, by his behavior, acts as if he never needs to apologize for anything and runs the home by dictatorial mandate. There is the pastor who is so blinded by his need for control and power that he has stifled the creative gifts of all those in the church and who speaks as though he is infallible. These too are examples of unconscious living.

Jesus encountered unconscious living. In fact, one of his last statements prior to his death involved those who live unconsciously. Referring to the mob who had cried out for his death, the soldiers who mocked and abused him and then crucified him, and the crowd of onlookers who ridiculed him as he hung dying our Lord prayed, "Father, forgive them, for they do not know what they are doing." They had discarded the light of the world—and they were completely unconscious of the fact.

The walk of life begins with an understanding of the unconscious life, and the desire and willingness to confront that unconsciousness. The more we live in unconsciousness the greater the number of unconscious snares we have in our lives. If an inferiority, for example, is conscious there is always the chance to correct it. Further, by constantly being in touch with other aspects of consciousness, it is subject to confrontation and change. If, however, the inferiority is repressed and isolated from consciousness, it can never be addressed and corrected. It becomes a part of the hidden baggage of the soul. From there, it thus has the potential of erupting into our behavior, usually when we least expect it. But that is not the worst of it. From the hidden cover of the shadow, the flaw becomes an unknown and unseen power broker in our life as it exerts its unconscious influence. "At all events," Jung wrote, "it forms an unconscious snag, thwarting our most well-meant intentions."[1]

As I have said, the point of departure of the walk of life is psychospiritual darkness. We are called to move out of darkness and to move ever toward the light. Initially this involves, as we have just seen, an understanding of the unconscious life and a willingness to address that unconsciousness. We do this as we confront the shadow, engaging in the spiritual warfare that this involves. Remember, the more we live unconsciously, the more powerful and pervasive the shadow becomes.

Confrontation of The Shadow

The greatest trick of the shadow is to convince us that there is no need to worry about all of this. This is to be expected. The shadow-side of our personality loathes the light and does not wish to be seen. (Remember Mr. Hyde?) The very fact that some aspect of our life has been split-off into the shadow gives evidence to the reality that this is something that we do not wish to face.

Confrontation of the shadow is the initial work we undertake toward a unified Self. As discussed in chapter three those aspects of the personality which are incompatible with one's embraced conscious attitude are disavowed and rejected. Consequently, they consolidate into a relatively independent splinter personality in the unconscious. As we

---

[1] C. G. Jung, *The Collected Works of C. G. Jung*, vol. 11, *Psychology and Religion: West and East*, 76-77.

confront the shadow, we undertake the work of integration and unification of the Self. That is, we move toward becoming a unified being. Recall that Jung considers encounter with the shadow to be the first step in the process toward individuation—that is, the first step toward coming to wholeness or spiritual and psychological maturity.

We confront our shadow, raise its contents to the level of consciousness by means of self-examination or self-analysis—an internal dialogue, if you will. A word of caution is in order here, however.

Earlier, I referred to the soldier known in the Vietnam war as the tunnel rat and compared the shadow to the maze of tunnels that coursed their way under the skin of the South Vietnam countryside. We must be careful—extremely careful, as we ferret about in our shadow. It is easy to get lost in the darkness of your own soul, easy to get lost within. The farther we go the darker, the more dangerous it gets. Furthermore, in this environment it is easy to make crucial mistakes. A suspected enemy could, in fact, be a friend—an ally. Something suspected of being detrimental to the psyche could in fact be a most important entity. Self-confidence, for example, could be mistaken for arrogance. A healthy skepticism that prevents one from being credulous could be mistaken for doubt and unbelief.

This is yet another reason why being involved in redemptive community is so vital. Others with whom we are united in the community can offer us insight into ourselves that we might miss because of personal blind spots or any other number of reasons.

One of the more useful tools the individual can employ as he confronts his shadow is dream work. We can learn a great deal about ourselves from our dreams, properly assisted by a trained therapist if need be. Because dreams arise out of the unconscious mind they can be an overlooked but vital ally in the encounter with the shadow. This is true because of a significant feature about our unconscious mind—a feature which I am convinced is there by the grace of God.

The unconscious mind has a tenacious tendency to tell us the truth about ourselves. If we can think of it in terms of proximity, the unconscious mind lies closer to the true Self than does the egocentric ego—that accepted part of us which we present to others. The accepted self (egocentric ego) is the persona we wish to present to the world. As such, it can be greatly detached from the Self. This is not the case with the unconscious mind however. The unconscious mind has what we call psychological integrity. It is genuine.

Because they emanate from the unconscious mind our dreams speak the truth about some aspect of us. This is why we should listen to what our dreams are trying to tell us. Let me illustrate this from a case study involving one of the most eerie dream sequences I have ever heard from a client.

I was seeing Bob and Mary, a couple in their mid-thirties who had been married for fifteen years, for marriage therapy. They were on the brink of divorce because of Bob's emotional detachment from Mary and their children and because he was having an ongoing affair with another woman—an affair he refused to give up.

Before terminating therapy (he did so after I suggested an interpretation to the following dream), Bob shared with me a recurring dream sequence he was having. These dreams were so vivid that he would wake up from them hyperventilating, covered in sweat and in utter panic. In the dream, Bob, Mary, and their four children were in their house. Bob would look to the window and notice a killer (his description) glaring in at the family. The sight of the killer would throw him into terror. The killer had a pitch-black face which was slightly shrouded. Further, there were no features to the face.

With the passing of time the killer came closer and closer in Bob's dream. (Not incidentally, at this same time Bob's behavior with the other woman was becoming brazen and the detachment from his family intensified.) First, the menacing figure came to the window, in later dreams, to the door, next into the house, and, in the final version, the killer was about to murder Mary. The killer approached Mary who was seated in a chair completely unaware of the ominous presence in the room. (Bob stated to me that he somehow knew that after killing his wife, the murderer intended to proceed upstairs and kill their children.) This was as far as the dream had progressed and each time it got to this point Bob would wake up in complete terror. Although he was very much aware that the killer was after his wife and children, at no time did the murderer approach Bob.

When he asked if I could shed some light on his dream, I told Bob that I thought I could but that I did not expect he would like what he would hear. He insisted that I go on. I explained to Bob, much as I discussed above, how the unconscious has a tenacious penchant for telling us the truth and how one way it attempts to do this is through our dreams. The interpretation I suggested to him was that the faceless killer in his dream was none other than Bob himself—or more precisely, his repressed shadow side. His subconscious was attempting to deliver a crucial message to Bob, namely, that his own behavior was threatening the very survival of his family. Further, just as the dream was rightly telling him, he alone could stop the killer. He alone could confront his shadow. What Bob was repressing, his unconscious mind was attempting to get him to face via the dream sequence.

Interestingly, Bob responded to my interpretation very politely, although his nonverbal cues sent a different message. I later found out that the moment he and Mary left my office he exploded in a fit of anger, dismissed me as a pathetic therapist, cursed and swore he would never come to me again—and he did not. Bob soon after left Mary and their four children and married the woman with whom he was having the affair.

Remember this about dreams: 1) they serve as a tool of the unconscious mind, 2) they tell the truth, 3) they show us some aspect of our shadow as it really is.

When we engage the shadow we are confronting that most primary and primal, most basic of all defense mechanisms, namely, repression. In the traditional psychoanalytic view, repression is considered the most primitive of all psychic defenses. It is the prototypical defense from which springs all others. When an individual confronts her shadow, she is striking at the very root of her fractured self—that which causes her to be fragmented and splintered.

It is therefore vitally important that we engage our shadow. It is in this action that we commence the work of becoming a unified Self. The farther we move into this work the more we cease to be divided and fragmented—which is the natural result of splitting our Self into acceptable and unacceptable parts.

I realize that regardless of how much emphasis is laid on the importance of encountering the shadow, there will be some who consider this work to be too hard, too risky, too time-consuming, or perhaps too esoteric to engage. Let me then make an appeal from another slant.

If we fail, for whatever reason, to confront the shadow, we affect more than just ourselves. What I am saying is this— failure to confront the shadow has an impact which transcends the individual himself. This principle is found in the words, "For none of us lives to himself alone and none of us dies to himself alone."

Dereliction of the parents to face their shadow results in the children taking upon themselves the shadow of their parents. Jung argued, and we must remember that this is no enemy of the church speaking, that children from religious families especially often fall into all sorts of vileness when their parents fail to challenge their shadow. Illustrating this from the lives of a Quaker family he knew Jung says, "The son became a thief and the daughter a prostitute. Because the father would not take on his shadow, his share of the imperfection of human nature, his children were compelled to live out the dark side which he had ignored."[1]

Of course, it is impossible to know whether or not Jung was correct in this specific example. However, his general principle gains credence from scripture which states that the children will "waste away" because of the sins of their parents. The prophet Jeremiah states this same concept with a rather imaginative twist saying, "The fathers have eaten sour grapes, and the children's teeth are set on edge."[2]

Let me illustrate. Jenny was a thirteen-year-old adolescent who was referred to me because of academic problems at school and oppositional behavior toward her parents. Jenny was not at all amenable to the idea of therapy. In fact, when her father brought her for the first session he had to argue with her for ten minutes outside my office before she finally consented to come in.

Jenny was a tough case. She was so brittle that I had to proceed very cautiously or risk having her refuse to continue therapy. After several sessions with Jenny I scheduled her parents for a consultation. In that session I voiced my concerns to them. I had seen kids like Jenny when I worked with adolescents in a psychiatric hospital. She was heading for a conduct disorder diagnosis in the not-too-distant future at this rate. As I talked with the parents, I explained to them that anger of Jenny's intensity is usually associated

---

[1] C. G. Jung, C. G. *Jung Speaking,* 158.

[2] Jer. 31:29.

with some sense of grave injustice—perceived or actual. We talked about this briefly.

Jenny's mother sat with head hung. Eventually she spoke. "I know why she is angry," she offered. As the story unfolded, Jenny's mother saw much about herself that she did not like and had never dealt with—shadow material—in her daughter. This caused her to distance herself from Jenny and to displace her attitude toward herself onto her daughter. This was the injustice Jenny was perceiving. It was the source of her fury. As her mother came to own her shadow she was able to undertake the work of integration. Furthermore, as her consciousness of the dynamics involved grew, Jenny's mother was then able to approach her daughter as a person in her own right, rather than as the personification of her own shadow. This was a classic example of a child *wasting away* because of the sins of her mother.

Remember the earlier maxim. The shadow will not be denied. If we insist on ignoring or denying our shadow we will run into it again and again in the lives of our children. And what we see there will repel us, causing us to reject the child and wound the relationship in the process.

To travel the walk of life is to pursue our psychospiritual growth. Like any travel, this critical journey has a point of departure. We commit ourselves to moving out of spiritual darkness by understanding and engaging the unconscious life and by confronting the shadow. As Fritz Perls puts it, "Every happy ending has to have a start." Forsaking spiritual darkness by this birth into spiritual life is the starting point to the happy ending that ultimately will characterize the walk of life.

Life is a continuous exploration of ever more reality. Life is a constant battle against everyone and anything that corrupts or diminishes its reality.[1]
—Eugene Peterson

CHAPTER 11

Into the Light

The walk of life is evolutionary. It is not the "sudden acquisition of wings," to use Peterson's nifty phrase.[2] The walk of life is the process of moving out of unconscious, spiritually dark living and growing into what we were created to be—of leaving behind the Shadowlands and moving toward individuation. As I have said, the walk of life is *the* essential purpose we all share. Let me demonstrate this from the words of Christ.

In the Sermon on the Mount our Lord elucidates this point about the preeminent role the walk of life is to hold for us. He says if we will pursue the walk of life, if we will give ourselves first and foremost to seeking the kingdom of God, then our Father would see to it that our daily needs in this life will be provided for.[3] Now, we must ask, why does Christ say this? Is he trying to barter with us or, worse, buy our devotion? Hardly. It is a promise of grace and goodness. What he is telling us is that life is too short to string our-

---

[1] Eugene Peterson, *Run With the Horses*, 24.

[2] Eugene Peterson, *Traveling Light: Reflections on the Free Life* (InterVarsity Press, 1982), 156.

[3] Mt. 6:25-34.

selves out, distracted with a hundred and one worrisome concerns. If we will but give ourselves to the *one thing*, he will take care of the *many* for us. "But seek first his kingdom and his righteousness, and all these things will be given to you as well," Jesus says.

There are two objectives to the walk of life that together comprise the destination toward which our journey takes us. These are 1) experiencing an ever-increasing consciousness and 2) psychospiritual maturity or individuation.

Consciousness—Living on Purpose

The walk of life involves a coming to consciousness. It is awakening to the rich, spiritual life to which we are called. In the previous chapter we saw in the early adult life of the Apostle Paul an example of unconscious living. Not until his encounter with the living Christ on the road to Damascus did he come to consciousness in his own life. Spiritually, he was born anew. Though temporarily blinded by that experience he could, for the first time, see. His spiritual eyes being opened, he was delivered from utter unconsciousness.

Before proceeding, I need to say a word about consciousness. There is a great deal of "conscious-raising psychobabble," to use John Leo's term, being spoken and written about today. (This ties in with the "new individualism" I will be talking about later.) This is a usage of the concept of consciousness that I wish to distance myself from. It operates as its own master, turning whatever it wishes to feel and experience into "reality."[1] This is pop-consciousness. The classic definition of reality is much less capricious. There is objective reality in both the physical and spiritual realms. The consciousness of which I am speaking is always

---

[1] We are all familiar with the adage "perception is reality." In an applied sense, there is some truth to this. In the larger picture, however, this cliché is untrue. Perception is perception. My perception of a thing *may be* reality-based but it is not automatically so merely because of my perception.

in terms of an increasing awareness of *that which is*. True consciousness addresses our relationship to actuality. Any consciousness I claim that does not do this is not consciousness at all—it is deception (self, or otherwise), or illusion.

The development of consciousness is like an ongoing and unfolding drama. Consciousness is not an attainment once achieved, like earning a bachelor's degree, for example. It is more like attempting the mastery of something. I recently heard Chet Atkins say that he just now felt that he was beginning to understand the guitar. Imagine that. Growth in consciousness is akin to this. It is a pursuit that will last us at least to the grave.

Again, consciousness addresses our relationship to actuality. The greater our consciousness, the more we are aware of and in harmony with not only this temporal world in which we live but with that greater reality, the realm of the spirit. "A spiritual kingdom lies all about us," writes Tozer, "altogether within reach of our inner selves, waiting for us to recognize it. God himself is here waiting our response to his presence."[1] Modernity has made a great mistake in equating the terms *visible* and *real*. There is a greater reality—greater in significance, duration, and intrinsic value—than the world of things which lies all around us and is observable to the human eye. Never make the mistake of believing that because the spiritual world is not visible it is not real. This is the chief error we can make. This simple truth—the greater reality of the invisible, spiritual world—is *Spirituality 101*. "So we fix our eyes," says Paul, "not on what is seen, but on what is unseen. For what is seen is temporary, but what is unseen is eternal."[2]

---

[1] A. W. Tozer, *The Pursuit of God* (Christian Publications, Inc., 1948), 52.
[2] 2 Cor. 4:18.

Once again, here is a place where participating in redemptive community can be of great assistance. We can encourage one another to keep our eyes fixed on things that matter so that we do not become sidetracked with peripheral issues. This will keep us from becoming "a spent pilgrim who has given up the journey and sits with a waxy smile trying to get what pleasure he can from sniffing the wilted flowers he has picked by the way."[1]

Individuation—Our Call to Psychospiritual Maturity

Our goal on the walk of life is psychospiritual growth toward what the New Testament calls "wholeness," (Jung's *individuation*). These terms are used to describe psychospiritual maturity, a term which itself begs to be defined. But first, it is important that we understand, as I say above, that psychospiritual maturity is not a punctiliar attainment. That is, we never get to the point where we can say "That's it. I have reached the finale." There is always more, much more. If we believe the New Testament, it is not until we reach the other side that we attain the total maturity, the completeness to which we are called and toward which we have begun our movement in this life.

My definition of wholeness or individuation (which, remember, refers to psychospiritual maturity) runs like this: *Individuation, or wholeness, is nothing less and nothing more than allegiance to the evolution, the unfolding of our unique, God-created Self.* This is what Christ is attempting to tell us when he says, "Therefore you shall be perfect, just as your Father in heaven is perfect." This is our lifelong calling.

Once again, we can see how sound theology and sound psychological theory are co-workers for the good of our lives.

---

[1] A. W. Tozer, *That Incredible Christian* (Christian Publications, Inc., 1964), 72.

The individuation Jung spoke of is in harmony with the wholeness ("perfect" above) Jesus calls us to. Recall once again Jung's definition of individuation:

> Individuation means becoming a single, homogeneous being, and, in so far as 'individuality' embraces our innermost, last, and incomparable uniqueness, it also implies becoming one's own self. We could therefore translate individuation as 'coming to selfhood' or 'self-realization.'[1]

As crucial as individuation is, Jung believed that few people ever attain it. I think he is right. Others agree. Scott Peck says:

> Most of us never totally complete the process and may never get very far at all. Most, to a greater or lesser degree, fail to individuate—to separate—ourselves from family, tribe, or caste. Even into old age we remain figuratively tied to the apron strings of our parents and culture. We are still dictated to by the values and expectations of our mothers and fathers. We still follow the direction of the prevailing wind and bow before the shibboleths of our society. We go with the crowd. From laziness and fear—fear of loneliness, fear of responsibility, and other nameless dreads—we never truly learn to think for ourselves or dare to be out of step with the stereotypes. But in light of all we understand, this failure to individuate is a failure to grow up and become fully human. For we are called to be individuals. We are called to be unique and different.[2]

There are several salient features within the idea of individuation. First, as we move further into wholeness we become more and more unified within ourselves. The technical term for this is homogeneity. The homogeneous person

---

[1] C. G. Jung, *The Collected Works of C. G. Jung*, vol. 7, *Two Essays on Analytical Psychology*, 13.

[2] M. Scott Peck, *The Different Drum*, 54.

has psychological integrity and congruity. She is narrowing that divide in her life that has her self segmented into accepted and unaccepted components. She is discovering how to confront her shadow—and is learning to embrace it.

The Danish theologian Søren Kierkegaard speaks to this. He tells us that "he who is not himself a unity is never really anything wholly and decisively; he only exists in an external sense."[1]

Second, and this is most important, there is no such thing as secular individuation. Secular individuation is an oxymoron—an impossible contradiction. Individuation is psychospiritual in nature and embraces our innermost Self.

If someone rejects the spiritual dynamic in life, he is left with a self that is incomplete, a self that is hopelessly truncated. There is no way individuation can be reached from that position. "I have treated many hundreds of patients," Jung states; "among all my patients in the second half of life—that is to say, over thirty-five—there has not been one whose problem in the last resort was not that of finding a religious outlook on life."[2]

This is precisely why a psychology which denies the spiritual aspects of life cannot possibly be a complete psychology. It does not confront the whole person. I am grateful to Scott Peck for the way he has championed this cause. Addressing the prestigious American Psychiatric Association in May, 1994, Dr. Peck stated,

> Although perhaps recently underestimated, the psychodynamic and social aspects of mental illness have held a respected place in the history of American psychiatry. *Its spiritual aspects, however, have not. Psychiatry has not only*

---

[1] Søren Kierkegaard, *Purity of Heart is to Will One Thing,* (Harper & Row, Publishers, 1956), 184.

[2] C. G. Jung, *Modern Man in Search of a Soul* (Harcourt, Brace, Jovanovich, Publishers, 1933), 229.

neglected but actively ignored the issue of spirituality.[1] (emphasis added)

Later in the same context Dr. Peck issues the warning that if American psychiatry continues to fail to address the spiritual dynamic of life, "it is likely to end up in an intellectual backwater." He is exactly right.

Let me hasten to say that in pointing out the essential spiritual nature of individuation or wholeness, I do not equate spirituality with organized religion and systemic dogma. Religion is not intrinsically so but in practice very often becomes at worst, the enemy of true spirituality and at best an impediment to it. I want to share the most vivid example I know of this with you. This is one of the most profound spiritual truths I have ever encountered. I hope it will shock you, and then make you think. This salient truth, which is drawn from the life of Jesus, can be stated like this: God walked this earth as man and was rejected by organized religion. Why? Because they deemed that he was not spiritual enough.

A third notable aspect of individuation is self-realization. In each of us there is a true Self—a God-created Self—which longs to develop. This is the Self we are born as and born to be. Ideally, as one grows into adolescence her chief task becomes that of identity formation, of detaching from mom and dad and embracing her own sense of "I" as this God-created Self develops and unfolds. She acquires her own boundaries—her own personal space. She begins to see in clearer focus that God-created Self as it begins to emerge. In terms of personal development, the balance of her life is spent in being true to that Self and working, by God's grace, to develop, to grow more and more into the fullness she was created to be.

---

[1] M. Scott Peck, *Further Along the Road Less Traveled* (Simon & Schuster, 1993), 233.

But something happens along the way. In a perfect world this God-created Self would develop normally. But this is not a perfected world. To varying degrees all of the influences in our early life are flawed. This primarily means of course our parents, who may have been everything from well intentioned but wrong in some crucial instances to hopelessly narcissistic or evil. What is more, as individuals we are flawed ourselves.

So what happens? This normal development of the Self gets skewed. For any number of pathological reasons detachment from the parents is flawed causing aspects of the God-created personality to be repressed, stifled, squelched into the shadow. The true Self is abandoned, its development arrested. From my perspective, I see this both psychologically and theologically as an act of treason. When this occurs, one has forsaken his highest calling, his greatest birthright. He has abandoned his God-created Self. This is the genesis of many if not most of our psychospiritual problems.[1] "Neurosis," Jung said, "is always a substitute for legitimate suffering."[2] Having abandoned the "legitimate suffering" we would encounter by being true to our God-created Self, all sorts of psychological hang-ups arise. The shadow and the ego-centric ego battle for control over the life we have abandoned. This is the original turf war.

I believe the resulting neuroses are God's calling card, his attempt to draw us back to the Self we were created to be. I hasten to add that I see these subsequent neuroses as *potentially* (depending on our response) more of a blessing

---

[1] The process of individuation must be parent-guided through childhood and early adolescence. This is *the* essential job of parenting. Ironically, most parents either cling to their children or prematurely withdraw from them, both of which hamper the individuation process.

[2] C. G. Jung, *The Collected Works of C. G. Jung*, vol. 11, *Psychology and Religion: West and East*, 75.

than a curse. They are God's effort to draw us back to our true Self—the God-created Self that resides deep within.

The fourth and last characteristic of individuation or wholeness I want to explain is related to self-realization which we have just discussed. I am referring to uniqueness. Woody Allen has said that his one regret in life is that he is not someone else! There is a lot of that going around. We have lost sight of our uniqueness—our incomparable one-of-a-kind-ness.

People are forever amazed over the fact that no two snowflakes are alike. Now, snowflakes are cool. Like everyone else, I too am fascinated by the fact that each one is unique. But a far greater wonder to me is the fact that each and every human being is original. This is true despite the fact that so many people are in a mad pursuit to forsake their Self and be someone else. When we do this, we surrender our uniqueness. This is a curious thing. When someone abandons her uniqueness she cannot simply stop living. So she begins to live her life like an actor on a stage—an actor playing the role of a well-defined individual—which, of course, is what she would have been all along if only she had chosen to live out her unique God-created Self!

I referred earlier to the Danish theologian Søren Kierkegaard. Kierkegaard wrote a book that should be required reading for every traveler on the walk of life. Although 150 years old, *Purity of Heart is to Will One Thing* is fresh and relevant enough today to be on the *New York Times* best-seller list. A hundred years before Jung developed his thoughts on individuation Kierkegaard wrote, "the consciousness before God of one's eternal responsibility to be an individual is that one thing necessary."[1]

There are three emphases in Kierkegaard's thesis: consciousness, responsibility, and individuality. We see these

---

[1] Søren Kierkegaard, *Purity of Heart is to Will One Thing*, 197-198.

same emphases in the psychology of Jung. And I have stressed their importance here.

Purity of Heart is one of the books in Kierkegaard's series *Edifying Addresses*. All of the *Addresses* are dedicated in the preface to "that solitary individual." The individual is the pervasive theme in Kierkegaard's writing. The burning question he presses again and again is "Do you now live so that you are conscious of yourself as an individual?" This is our calling. This is our lifelong responsibility.

We may bristle at these words of Kierkegaard. On the surface they sound audacious, even brazen. "Who is this man," we might ask, "that he dare tell us what purity of heart is? How could he presume to say such a thing?" But let us consider Kierkegaard's point for a moment. He says that purity of heart is the consciousness before God of one's eternal responsibility to be an individual—to be true to the Self. I honestly do not see how we can disagree with this—or why we would want to. This affirms our uniqueness, our dignity, our significance. Kierkegaard is right. It is surely a sign of depravity, if not lunacy, to hold the position that it is better to lose yourself in the mass of humanity, wandering about as an amorphous being, or to don the actor's mask and play the role of a person, rather than to individuate, to embrace our God-created Self and to, in fact, *be* a person.

The kind of person Kierkegaard is speaking of—those who are pure in heart—do not deny their individuality, they come to embrace it. They do not abandon their sacred Self in order only to live an actor's life. Such a person possesses the courage and commitment essential for authentic living; they possess the courage to be.

Although I trust the tenor of this book has made it clear all along, perhaps this would be a good time to pause and discuss the kind of individualism that I am *not* talking about. I am not talking about the kind of rugged individualism Herbert Hoover spoke of in his campaign speeches. This type of individualism stresses a kind of self-sufficiency that is not altogether helpful. As long as a person strives to be this type of individual, I do not believe she can ever experience redemptive community. Nor do I believe she can proceed very far in her psychospiritual development.

This type of individuality is not terribly healthy. Really, it is not individuality at all, it is isolationism. It is not the individuality of growing more and more to be our God-created Self. Rugged individualism results in extreme loneliness. This is why our cities have been described as a place where millions of people are lonely together. True individuality recognizes the truths of dependence and interdependence as well as that of independence.

This is the first type of false individualism and we might call it the old individualism. There is another type however, just as false, but more prevalent today. It is just as erroneous as the old. We can refer to this as the new individualism.

The new individualism is in vogue in our society today and is cut from the same cloth as the pop-consciousness I spoke of earlier. In books, seminars, and talk shows this new individualism has become a cottage industry. This is the "I gotta be me" kind of individuality. It is infantile and narcissistic. It is superficial. This individualism champions rights all the day long but says nary a word about responsibility. This is individualism gone mad. In fact, it is not individualism at all. It is self-absorption.

Sociologist Daniel Yankelovich gives a perfect example of this "I gotta be me" type of pseudo individualism:

> A psychologist friend told me an anecdote which had amused—and bemused—her. A patient in psychotherapy with her, a woman in her mid-twenties, complained that she had become nervous and fretful because life had

173

grown so hectic—too many big weekends, too many discos, too many late hours, too much talk, too much wine, too much pot, too much lovemaking.

"Why don't you stop?" asked the therapist mildly. Her patient stared blankly for a moment, and then her face lit up, dazzled by an illumination.

"You mean I really don't have to do what I want to do?" she burst out with amazement.[1]

It boggles the mind.

The mantra of the new individualism (borrowing heavily from Abraham Maslow's notion of self-actualization) is self-fulfillment. This, according to the new individualism, is what life is all about. Walk into any bookstore and you will instantly see how popular this doctrine is. The doctrine of the new individualism will eventually be seen for what it is—a bankrupt philosophy. Unfortunately, this realization, when it comes, is going to leave behind a lot of disillusioned people. Yankelovich is right. It is time that we step off Maslow's escalator. There is a better way.

We do not need the old individualism nor the new individualism. Both are destitute. What we need, what we are called to, is *true* individualism. This is the individualism Christ calls us to when he bids us follow him. It is the kind championed by Kierkegaard, and Jung—the kind I have sought to vivify in this book.

True individualism does not focus on self-fulfillment (of the popular type) but on self-transcendence. This is a seminal reality. True individualism calls us to a greater purpose—a higher purpose. As we engage in the walk of life, the journey toward individuation or psychospiritual completeness, we are increasingly liberated from the unconscious shadow life. We are delivered from the sturdiest of all prisons, the lifeless old nature. True individualism is a lifelong

---

[1] Daniel Yankelovich, *New Rules* (Random House, 1981), 85-86.

work of regeneration from the inside out. This is miles removed from the new individualism (and the old for that matter) which is ego based. This is not selfhood at all. It is idolatry. Again, it is individualism gone mad.

Yet, there is a great mystery and paradox at work here. When one commits himself to true individualism—to living out his God-created Self—he runs into self-fulfillment. It is a fruit of the process but never the goal. "For whoever desires to save his life will lose it, and whoever loses his life for my sake will find it." Funny how life works.

So then, here is our purpose, our great vocation. We are called to commence the walk of life, if we have not already done so, and to persevere on if we have. Sound too simple? A notorious bank robber asked when he was finally captured why he robbed banks. "Because that's where the money is," he replied. Ray Charles was once asked in a television interview what was the worst thing about being blind. His answer? "You can't see." Some things are just that simple. I believe that this is true of life. Its essential principles are simple. They are simple—but they are not *easy*. Never confuse the two terms. "Love your neighbor as yourself," Christ says. Now, we can all grasp this. A child can understand it. But doing it. Ah, that is the hard thing. "Confess your sins to each other," we are told. Now, you understand these words. So do I. But do you practice them? Do I? God help us, that's hard! "I don't give a fig for the simplicity this side of complexity," said Oliver Wendell Holmes, "but I would die for the simplicity on the other side of complexity." Exactly.

To strive for individuation is to do the hard work necessary to move toward wholeness. Make no mistake, it is hard work. I believe this is exactly why we do not pursue our own growth with more ardor—because the work is not easy. Again, laziness is the great enemy of psychospiritual development.

The walk of life is evolutionary. It is a journey out of and away from something and into and toward something. The walk of life is out of the shadow and away from unconscious living. It is into consciousness and toward individuation or psychospiritual wholeness. The walk of life is a journey of redemption and restoration. It is the reclaiming of our birthright—all that was lost in the fall. The walk of life is difficult but it is imminently rewarding. It can be scary, but it builds courage and inner strength. The walk of life involves a kind of death but it opens before us an even greater and richer life. It can be exasperating, exhausting, confusing, painful, and perilous. But it is worth every step we take. And when we are on the walk of life, not a single step is taken unaccompanied.

Part Six

WE ARE NOT ALONE

We must remember two things about promises: 1) a promise is only as good as the character of the individual making it, and 2) it is only as good as the ability of that individual to deliver.

CHAPTER 12

The Word of a Gentleman

In a different day, business deals in this country were sealed with a handshake. This was known as a gentleman's agreement. A gentleman, a lady could be relied upon to keep his or her word because a person's pledge was the ambassador for their character. And folks took this seriously. The promises of God are like that. We can trust them because they are the words of a gentleman.

The promises of God are not illusory. They are not wish-based fantasy ropes that delusional people cling to. Quite the contrary. "God's promises conform to reality, and whoever trusts them enters a world not of fiction but of fact," wrote Tozer. Indeed.

Promises are wonderful things. Or, at least, they can be. I have no doubt that for some readers the very mention of the word raises mixed feelings. The mind goes back to the father who kept promising you a bicycle when you were a boy—a bicycle that never came. It travels back to the mother who promised repeatedly to spend more time with you—but never delivered.

You see, a promise is only as good as the character of the individual making it and the ability of that individual to deliver. Why can we trust the promises of God? Well, for one thing, because he has the power to deliver the goods. But more importantly, we can trust his promises because his character is at stake—his good name is on the line. God's promises are his oath, his sacred vow to us, and he is as good as his word. There are two promises from God that stand like guardian angels ever ready to assist the traveler as she proceeds down the walk of life. The promises are: 1) the oath of presence and 2) the oath of meaning.

The Oath of Presence

The first promise is recorded in the Epistle to the Hebrews as a simple couplet: "Never will I leave you; never will I forsake you."[1] Peterson translates the verse like this: "I'll never let you down, never walk off and leave you."

A little background is useful to help us understand this promise. The book of Hebrews was written to a redemptive community that was being hammered by its culture. They were being persecuted, though not to the point of death (12:4). Some in the ranks had abandoned the walk of life and many more were in danger of doing so. The book was written to encourage the believers to resist the temptation to abandon the walk and to press on. In the midst of one of the many passages of encouragement the writer stops and reminds them of the promise of God's enduring presence: "Never will I leave you; never will I forsake you."

I say the writer reminded them of this promise because, as Jewish believers, it was one they had certainly heard before. It is a promise with roots sunk deep in the annals of

[1] Heb. 13:5.

Hebrew history. It hearkens back to a time just as ominous as that being faced by the author's first-century readers—a turbulent time in the young nation of Israel. Their leader, Moses, is near death. The people face the greatest challenge they have yet encountered since leaving the bondage of Egypt on their journey to the Land of Promise. (A fitting name for it!) They are a band of pilgrims engaged in their own walk of life.

Moses has told them of his imminent death. The anxiety level is high as they sit camped on the bank of the River Jordan. The land is theirs—but they must take it. (This is one of the central paradoxes of the walk of life.) There are enemies to fight, battles to be waged. To say the people are scared and uncertain is an understatement. What's more, in this most pivotal of times they are about to get a new leader. Joshua, Mose's young understudy, is about to take the helm. This only adds to their anxiety.

In one of his last addresses to his beloved redemptive community—to those he had both led and joined on the walk of life—Moses spoke these words: "Be strong and courageous. Do not be afraid or terrified because of [the enemies], for the LORD your God goes with you; *he will never leave you nor forsake you.*"[1] (emphasis added)

You see, all travelers on the walk of life share common struggles. We get confused, intimidated, overwhelmed by the challenge of it all. This is nothing new. But the promise is there. And to trust that promise is reality-based behavior. "Never will I leave you," says the Master, "never will I forsake you."

This is the promise of the critical hour. It is the assurance needed most when we feel overpowered and under-equipped at any given stage of the journey. It is the

---

[1] Deut. 31:6.

promise that assuages our fears or at the very least, helps us fight through them.

This is an important promise for our spiritual pilgrimage because of the nature of individuation. While it is true that we share in the interdependence of redemptive community the fact is we ultimately stand as a solitary individual. While we share in a common point of departure and a common destination, our journey is our own. It is as the old hymn puts it: we walk a lonesome valley, we walk it by our self, and nobody else can walk it for us.

With consciousness comes increased potential for loneliness because of the growing awareness that ultimately we are alone. This is why the promise before us is invaluable. While it is true that no other human can share our personhood, God can. His Spirit resides within the personality of the spiritually alive. And he will never leave us—never abandon us.

This promise embodies one of the most if not *the* most emphatic statements in the Bible. In the grammar of the Greek text of this promise (the language in which the epistle was originally written) there are five negative particles used. It is as if God is saying "I will never, never, never, never, never abandon you."[1] It makes for poor translation but what a promise!

The Oath of Meaning

The second of our two promises is, like the first, essential to the traveler on the walk of life. It states, "And we know that in all things God works for the good of those who love him, who have been called according to his purpose."[2]

---

[1] For anyone interested or curious, the negative particles are "οὐ μή—οὐδ᾽ οὐ μή."

[2] Rom. 8:28.

Joseph Goebbels was Hitler's diabolical minister of propaganda. He was a master at manipulating the masses through lies. He had an interesting, if sordid, insight into lying. Goebbels said that the problem with most of the lies told is that they are not big enough. The grander the scale of the lie, the more apt people are to believe it, he taught. That period of German history seems to bear his thesis out.

This set me to thinking the other day, in relation to our present subject. Why is it that we seem more willing to believe grand lies than grand truths? This is so even when the one giving the promise is God—and therefore it is *his* character and *his* reputation on the line. This is a conundrum to me. To be candid, I would find the promise of Romans 8:28 much easier to believe if it were not quite so grand. I mean, it's just the scope of the thing. Why are we (I trust I am not the only one!) like this?

We may wish that we could pare the thing down a bit but there it stands. "And we know that in all things God works for the good of those who love him, who have been called according to his purpose."

Some preliminary remarks are in order to prevent two grave misconceptions. First, this promise does not say that all things that come our way *are* good. I have seen people make this error of thought with some bad consequences. They lose a child in a tragic death and mistakenly think they are somehow supposed to view this tragedy as a good thing. They find that their spouse of so many loving years has terminal cancer and they errantly believe they are supposed to find a way to declare this good.

No. Look carefully at the wording. This promise does not tell us that all things *are* good. Rather, it says that all things *work together* for good. This is the operative phrase. I will return to this shortly.

Second, do not be concerned by the phrase referring to God's call. I have had more than one spiritual neophyte approach me because they were confused and not a little disturbed by this phrase. "What if I am not one of the called?" they ask. This is a very easy anxiety to dispel. Look at the antecedent clause. It says "to those who love God." Do you love God? You would not be on the walk of life seeking spiritual development if you did not.

But perhaps you have not commenced the walk. Then ask yourself this. Am I willing to start the journey? Am I hungry for more than the life of the five senses? This is his call to your true Self. Respond to that inner voice. Commence the walk. To love God is to move toward him and respond to his voice.

Returning to the promise before us let me start by saying that the walk of life is sometimes messy. It does not consist solely of beautiful glades and fields of heather. There are creeks and swamps to cross. There is mud—and muck. There are not only the balmy days of sunshine but also the windswept, rainy, damp days that chill to the bone. In short, life is hard. The walk of life is hard. We trip, we stumble, we fall. There are things which come our way that we can do absolutely nothing about but that we are expected to do something with—things which are not intrinsically good or valuable in and of themselves. Added to all of this is the (probably daily) fact that we just flat screw up. I am to believe that all of this stuff is somehow suppose to work together toward some grand good? Well, yes. Do you see what I meant earlier? It would be much easier if the promise were not quite so big.

The potential this promise holds for relieving a thousand and one little neuroses is utterly fantastic. What worries, fears, shames, embarrassments, failures, might straightway be chased from our minds if this promise were embraced aright—if we understood that despite our origins, our goofs and gaffs, our sins and stumbles, and the many times we have lost our way on the walk of life—there is a sovereign God who is weaving all together for our good? It is as though we feel we do not have the right to such a promise. Again, it is just too big.

Of course it goes without saying (but I have long since learned that that which goes without saying had better be said) that this promise is not meant to provide a guarantee to those who have no interest in spiritual development.[1] This is a promise to a certain people, as the wording makes very clear. It is God's vow to those on the walk of life.

Because we are creatures of time we live in the moment. We lose sight of the overall picture. God, on the other hand, works on the wide loom. Those things which we may think of as our greatest failures, our worst defeats, our saddest days may turn out to be the very thing God uses most. These are the dark threads the weaver needs. They give hue and texture to the tapestry of our life. Our development, such as it would be, would be bland and one-dimensional without them.

We have the deposition of a famous and important individual as an example of this promise. The man who is about to share his story with us was, at the time of the telling, the prime minister of the most powerful nation on earth. His name is Joseph Bar-Jacob.[2]

The story of Joseph is a remarkable study. He was a gifted young man from a wealthy family. Joseph was one of those people who just seemed to those around him to be destined for greatness. Further, he was the favorite child of his father because Joseph was born to him when he was an old man. Because of his giftedness (about which he was not

---

[1] But let that person who heretofore has shown no interest in her spiritual development commence the walk of life and she will have a pervasive awareness that God has been at work all along. This is a great mystery.

[2] See Genesis 37-50.

a little insolent) and the fact that he was his father's favorite son, he was hated by his numerous older brothers. So great was their hatred for Joseph that they plotted to murder him. At the time, Joseph was a seventeen-year-old adolescent. One of the brothers, smitten more by commerce than conscience said "Wait! There's no profit in killing him. Lets sell him into slavery and we can make a few bucks." Talk about sibling rivalry!

Joseph was sold, literally, to a trade caravan traveling to Egypt. Upon arrival in Egypt he was once again sold, this time to a high-ranking Egyptian military official named Potiphar. In fact, this man who had just purchased Joseph was captain of the pharaoh's guard—no small position.

Joseph rose to stature in Potiphar's house because of his excellent character and managerial skills. Potiphar had placed supervision of his entire estate in Joseph's hands. By now, Joseph had grown into a handsome, well-built young man. Potiphar's wife, had not failed to notice this. One day, while her husband was away, she seduced Joseph. "Come to bed with me!" she coaxed. Joseph refused. He explained to her that he could not be disloyal to the master who had placed such confidence in him. Potiphar's wife was undeterred. Alone in the house she grabbed him by his clothing saying yet again, "Come to bed with me!" Joseph pulled out of his cloak and ran out of the house.

I do not know if it is true in general that "Hell hath no fury like a woman scorned" but it was certainly true in this instance. Being insulted by Joseph's rejection she cried "RAPE!" Imagine the scene. Imagine the talk in the servants' quarters. Potiphar's wife framed Joseph and then lied to her husband about the whole thing upon his return.

Falsely accused, Potiphar threw Joseph into prison. Even there his excellence was noted. The prison warden put him in charge of the other prisoners.

We flash forward in the story two years. The pharaoh had a disturbing dream regarding a coming famine, although at the time he did not know the dream's interpretation. The king's cupbearer, himself a former prisoner, recalled that Joseph had a knack for interpreting dreams and told this to pharaoh. Upon hearing this, pharaoh summoned Joseph from prison. He was summarily cleaned up and brought before the most politically powerful man in all the world, the pharaoh of Egypt. Joseph interpreted the dream and suggested to the pharaoh what he should do to prepare for the coming famine. So impressed by Joseph is pharaoh, and so grateful for his insight, that he exalts him to the position of prime minister. Joseph is now the second most politically powerful individual in all the world.

Flash forward again. The famine of which the pharaoh dreamed (which Joseph interpreted) is now full-blown. Because of the preparation undertaken by Joseph's wise leadership, Egypt is faring well through the tough times. Not so for her neighbors. One day a group of travelers arrives from the north seeking to buy food. They are Joseph's brothers long forgotten. He recognizes them but they do not know him. Joseph has grown up. And the powerful man that they now stand before in all his regalia is quite different from the lad they had sold into slavery.

After a series of intriguing encounters Joseph revealed himself to his brothers. They were smitten with guilt—and then terror. They were standing before the man whose power was exceeded by only one other person in the world—and as a teenager they had sold him into slavery! To say the least, they feared for their lives. Now listen carefully to the words of this great man: "Don't be afraid. Am I in the place of God? *You intended to harm me, but God intended it for good to accomplish what is now being done,* the saving of many lives. So then, don't be afraid. I will provide for you and your children." (emphasis added)

Joseph recognized the greater reality, the reality of the promise of meaning. Everything that had transpired in his life was being woven together by God for a grander purpose. Joseph did not say that it was great to be sold as a slave by his own brothers, that it was terrific to be falsely accused of attempted rape, that it was just swell to rot in prison for two years. What he is saying is that the sovereign God cannot be thwarted by such things and that he has woven it all together into one incredible life. The worst intentions of Satan and man together cannot tie the omnipotent hands of God.

As a practicing therapist I meet so many people who are literally poisoned in their soul over the injustices and bad breaks that have come their way. They can name the person, place, and time of every wrong they have suffered. They have never forgiven, they have never forgotten—and for some, it is likely that they never will. Believing the promise before us is the great antidote for the soul thus poisoned.

Joseph could have slain his brothers on the spot. He had the political authority to do so. But he realized in the very marrow of his being the truth of this pilgrim's promise. Actually, he told them something after he had revealed himself to them, that causes me to chuckle. He said: "And now, do not be distressed and do not be angry with yourselves for selling me here, because it was to save lives *that God sent me ahead of you.*" (emphasis added)

"That God sent me ahead of you?" I mean, what an outlook! I can hear me. I would have recounted every little detail of my ordeal starting with their little capital gain obtained by selling my tail into slavery. (Do you realize how *that* could effect your self-esteem? Having your own brothers sell you into slavery!) They would have heard it all! I'm just not quite that far down the walk of life yet. The difference between how I would have reacted and how Joseph did react lies in the degree to which this promise was engrafted into the very fibre of his being and the degree to which it is not yet engrafted into mine.

Think of Mariah's story, in chapter seven. If there is such a thing as a right to have a poisoned soul then, like Joseph, this lady has it. But, although she still struggles from time to time, she is not about to give in to her dark side. She believes the promise.

I do not for one minute pretend to understand how all this works. But I am not in the least troubled by that fact. (I do not really understand how television works either but that does not prevent me from watching the football game.) It is quite comforting to have a God greater than my comprehension.

But we long to understand what we can. This is a healthy desire and I have no doubt that it is of God. So let me try to assist our understanding of this promise, if I may, from the world of chemistry. The atoms of sodium and chlorine turn into ions by the giving or receiving of an atomic particle. When these ions join together they form what is known as an ionic compound. In this case, the compound formed is called sodium chloride ($NaCl$). This particular ionic compound is more stable than the two elements (sodium and chlorine) from which it is formed. Sodium is a silvery metal that reacts violently when it comes in contact with certain substances. Chlorine is a poisonous gas. Sounds like the potential for a volatile brew. However, combine this potentially violent sodium atom with this poisonous chlorine atom and a remarkable thing occurs. You get table salt.

In some little way, I think this helps us understand the promise of Romans 8:28. Events in our lives that alone can be potentially dangerous, even disastrous, God, like a master chemist, combines into something wonderful. This is the synergism[1] taking place in the life of one who is committed

---

[1] Indeed, the words translated as "work together" is the Greek word from which we get the term synergism (sunergei).

to his psychospiritual development.

One final word about this promise. I am not sure that our greatest problem with it is a lack of trust. I think our greater problem may be that of control—an issue at which this promise strikes at the very heart. We want control. We want to be able to control what takes place in our lives and are more than a little distressed that we do not have it. Even though deep down most of us realize that we have precious little control in life, we prefer to think that we do. It seems that we prefer the illusion that we are in control to the reality that God is.

The Oath of Presence, and the Oath of Meaning—as we travel the walk of life these two promises travel with us like, as I said earlier, guardian angels. They assure us first that although our journey is solitary, we are never alone. Our Lord is with us—his very Spirit residing within. Second, we have the promise that all we encounter, all we experience, all we do as we journey on—God himself is weaving together for the good of our psychospiritual development.

There must be in you a living faith and
trust that the Lord wishes to give you all
that you need . . . for your good.[1]
—Lorenzo Scupoli

CHAPTER 13

The Pilgrim's Provisions

Living near the Smoky Mountains for so long, I have done a fair bit of hiking. You can always spot an inexperienced hiker by his provisions. Either he will have too many or too few or the wrong kind. Over the years I have seen some pretty funny things. There is the guy who loads a cross-country pack with about thirty pounds of gear for a day trip. Another hiker will plan to climb a rocky bluff but she will be wearing casual shoes instead of hiking boots. I have been with friends on overnight trips who thought because it was summer they would need nothing but the clothes on their back. You could not convince them that, even in the summer, high in the mountains the night temperature bites.

Likewise, you can tell instantly when a hiker has made proper provisions for the journey. His provisions are neither too great nor insufficient. He knows what he needs and takes exactly that. A seasoned hiker has a proper appreciation for the importance of provisions.

Provisions are important for the walk of life. It is a long, arduous journey. The traveler must be well equipped.

---

[1] Lorenzo Scupoli, "Of Prayer" in *An Anthology of Devotional Literature*, comp. Thomas A. Kepler (Baker Book House, 1977), 290.

There are six provisions which are absolutely essential to the pursuit of psychospiritual development. We will not make it far down the road to individuation without them. The essential provisions are faith, hope, love, grace, mercy, and peace.

Faith

It is important to distinguish between two types of faith before proceeding. There is common faith and there is existential faith. Nothing in all the world is more abundant than common faith. When you go to your favorite restaurant, you have faith in the chef that he is not going to poison you. When you go to the druggist, you have faith that she is not going to encapsulate strychnine instead of your antibiotic and give it to you. On and on these illustrations go. Common faith is so common that we are seldom ever even conscious of it. This is not the kind of faith before us. The faith I am talking about is existential faith—the faith that is inexorably linked to our human existence.

I want to move rapidly to say that I know the uneasiness the word faith stirs in some. Faith has been widely employed by many who are simply copping-out on life. It has been manipulated to excuse some of the most foolish behavior imaginable.[1] Others have had such a bad experience with organized religion that they never want to hear the term again. Frankly, my experience leads me to believe that those who talk about it the most sometimes practice it the least. So, if you are one of those people for whom the word faith is a turn-off, please give me a chance to refresh your opinion of the word before you tune out.

When I speak of faith I do not at all mean to imply adherence to some sterile creed or dogma. Nor do I mean mental ascent to some body of doctrine. This is what most

---

[1] A. W. Tozer says "Faith never means gullibility. The man who believes everything is as far from God as the man who refuses to believe anything."

often passes for faith in organized religion—and it misses
the boat. Faith is the energy of the spiritual life. "Faith en-
ables our spiritual sense to function," writes Tozer. "Where
faith is defective the result will be inward insensibility and
numbness toward spiritual things." Faith is that which answers the call to the walk of life.

Jung addresses this very fact and confirms it. Recall, as
discussed earlier, that he says of the hundreds of patients he
treated over the age of thirty-five there had not been one
whose problem was not that of finding a spiritual outlook
on life. "And none of them has been really healed," he adds,
"who did not regain his religious outlook."[1]

Jung does not stop here. The farther he goes the more
troubling his words become for those who reject the spiritual life:

> It seems to me, that, side by side with the decline of
> religious life, the neuroses grow noticeably more frequent.
> . . . Among my patients from many countries, all of them
> educated persons, there is a considerable number who
> came to see me, not because they were suffering from a
> neurosis, but because they could find no meaning in life.[2]

This is tough to swallow for the secular Western mind. It
prefers to worship at the shrine of empirical validity. But it
is so nonetheless.

"Without faith it is impossible to please God," we are
told. Why is that? Is God just being difficult? Hardly. Faith
is the means by which we lay hold of the spiritual realm.
The spiritual world is vivid, but it is only entered and ac-
cessed by faith. The New Testament states it so marvelously:
"The fundamental fact of existence is that this trust in God,
this faith, is the firm foundation under everything that makes
life worth living."[3]

---

[1] C. G. Jung, *Modern Man in Search of a Soul*, 229.

[2] Ibid., 230-231.

[3] Heb. 11:1, *THE MESSAGE*.

Faith is one of the rudimentary provisions for the journey. No one has ever begun the walk of life without it. Not strong faith perhaps, not solid faith maybe—but the faith is there. It may at first be no hardier than the legs of a newborn fawn. But that is okay. It is the object of the faith that matters most, not the muscularity of it.

Hope

The second provision is hope. Although faith and hope are two different entities, they always occur in tandem. You never find one without the other; they are inexorably linked. When hope expires, it always takes faith with it. Likewise, faith always produces hope. In *Pilgrim's Progress*, Bunyan's classic, the first traveling companion Christian meets is Faithful. The second is Hopeful. Along his journey Christian is imprisoned by the Giant Despair in the dungeon within his Doubting Castle. Despair and doubting, the natural enemies of faith and hope. The two are inseparable.

I remember in graduate school reading a chilling account which indelibly stamped on my mind the psychological importance of hope. During the Korean War, Chinese experts were brought in to torture—using psychological warfare—a group of American POWs. The soldiers were put through an incredible regimen of mental torment which focused on their thoughts about their wives, children, and parents. They were told that their wives had written them off as dead and had taken new lovers. They were told that their children were now calling another man "daddy." They were made to believe that their parents had forgotten them. And a remarkable, incredibly sad thing began to happen. The POWs in this group began to die. Subsequent autopsies revealed no medical reason for their decease. They just laid down and died. It was psychologically induced homicide. They died from a loss of hope.

Modern man and woman are in the same boat as these tragic prisoners. They are dying from lack of hope. Driving through town the other day I saw an old dilapidated pick-up truck with a bumper sticker that illustrated the resignation so common today. It read, "Caution. Driver just doesn't give a shit anymore." Despair is the place where hope goes to die.

Hope is what reminds us that it is all worth it. The hope of leaving the Shadowlands behind, the hope of growing in consciousness, the hope of individuation and psychospiritual wholeness, the hope of a rich and full life. Hope is what energizes us to persevere when the going gets rough.

In the New Testament the word most commonly translated "hope" always carries the meaning of "the expectation of something good." We would expect that. God is a good God. Recall the second promise we looked at in the previous chapter. "All things work together *for good*." The psalmist tells us "No *good thing* will he withhold from those who walk his paths." How wonderful a gift hope is; and how necessary as we move down the path toward individuation.

Once again, we are at a place where involvement in a redemptive community can be invaluable. We can encourage one another when hope falters.

Love

The third of our pilgrim's provisions is love. I must confess. I am so very tired of this word love. Not the concept mind you, just the word. It has been so overworked and used to describe so many different things, that for me it has lost virtually all of its power. Much of this has to do with the poverty of the English language. The ancient Greeks had four words for love. We have the one.

Another problem for me as we talk about love is the vastness of the subject. It overwhelms me. I can, for example, say to you that "God loves you." But it is a theme so vast that I am swallowed up in it and can say little more in addition of any real value. If I try to expand upon that statement I am just plain overmatched. Oh, to be sure, I can give you evidence of his love for you (at least I think I can), but I cannot explain the matter. Let me illustrate.

I once attended a lecture where the speaker was amplifying some point by referring to an experience recently come his way. He had taken a friend who had not traveled more than a few miles from his place of birth in Oklahoma, on a trip with him to California. The experience of flight had blown the guy's mind. Seeing Los Angeles had the same effect on him. He had experienced nothing like any of this in his simple rural life. The speaker said that he decided to show his friend the Pacific Ocean—among other reasons, just to see his reaction. The man was speechless. Never in his life had he imagined such a sight. As they were about to leave the man said to his host, "Just a minute." He ran down to the shore, waded out a few feet, bent over to do something, and then returned.

When he got back up to the car he had a jar of water in his hand. "What in the world is that for?" the host asked. His friend responded, "My family has never seen anything like this ocean. I want to take this back and show them what the ocean is like."

That is my predicament as I try to describe the love God has for us. At the very best, I can but scoop out a jar full and say "Look at this!" It's inadequate; I know.

We only begin the walk of life, only have any interest in it at all because God has not left us alone to be swallowed up by the Shadowlands. The very thing that set me on the walk of life some twenty-six years ago was my encounter with this fact—the fact of God's love, as he made me conscious of it through the following words:

This is how much God loved the world: He gave his Son, his one and only Son. And this is why: so that no one be destroyed; by believing in him, anyone can have a whole and lasting life. God didn't go to all the trouble of sending his Son merely to point an accusing finger, telling the world how bad it was. He came to help, to put the world right again.[1]

This was exactly what I wanted. To begin the process of being made whole, to be put right again. I began my spiritual journey. I joined the walk of life.

God first loved us, giving us the ability and the desire to love him in return. "We, though, are going to love—love and be loved. First we were loved, now we love. He loved us first."[2]

We are not only to experience the love of God—and to love him in return. We are also to love ourselves. Like consciousness and individualism discussed in chapter ten, this is a subject that has taken a lot of abuse in recent years. Self-esteem is all the rage.

When I talk of self-love however, I mean, just as with the issues in chapter ten, to distance myself a great deal from the popular sacrament of self-esteem. While I suppose a good number of people have benefitted from the self-esteem movement, I think the detriments outweigh the benefits on the balance. I agree with Robyn Dawes of Carnegie Mellon University who calls self-esteem "the Holy Grail of pop psychology."

Let me add that we are again dealing with the poverty of language. Many people who talk about self-esteem have in mind precisely what I am calling self-love. The self-esteem that has become so popular—the movement—is different altogether. So I am going to propose new terminology. The psychospiritually healthy quality is what I refer

---

[1] John 3:16-17, *THE MESSAGE.*
[2] 1 Jn. 4:19, *THE MESSAGE.*

to as self-love. The narcissistic self-regard so popular today I call self-absorption.

Self-absorption is preoccupation with self. As I alluded earlier, there is not a dime's worth of difference between it and narcissism. Self-absorption is preoccupied with (though, not so brazenly stated) one question: "What makes me feel good?" Acts of self-sacrifice are common in love. The self-absorbed person does not make such sacrifices. They do not feel good.

My greatest problem with the self-absorbed type of self-esteem however is that it is another example of living by proxy. It is vicarious living in the most subtle sense. The God-created Self still loses out; it is still held captive. The only difference being that here, the jailor is the ego, not the shadow. Self-absorption does not focus on the Self and what is best for the Self. Rather, its fixation is on what makes the egocentric ego feel good. Everyone and everything is filtered by the self-absorbed person on the basis of how they or it scores on this single question: "How does this person or this thing make me feel?"

Self-love is radically different from self-absorption. Grounded in unseen realities its focus is first and foremost on the psychospiritual development of the self and others. Self-love asks the question "What is best?" That which is best is by no means always easy and by no means always feels good. To the contrary, true self-love must often say, "My feelings be damned," and then go on and do what must be done.

Self-love is healthy and crowns our life with the dignity that was lost in the fall. How can it possibly bring honor to our Creator if we have contempt for that which he made—our God-created Self? The whole passion of Christ is about showing us that we are of inestimable value to the Father.

Finally, we are to love one another. "Love your neighbor as you love yourself," we are told. This sentence is in the imperative mode meaning that it is a command. This lays to rest the greatest misconception about love, namely, that love is primarily an emotion. Actually, Christ takes it even a step further. "Love your enemies," he tells us. If love were primarily an emotion, there is no way he could say this to us. You cannot give a command to emotions. If that were possible I could make millions curing depressed clients. I would merely command them: "Feel enthusiastic." People from around the world would be lined up outside my office door.

But do you know what is the interesting thing? We really do love our neighbor as (i.e., in the same way) we love our self. Someone who regards herself with loathing treats others with loathing. Have you ever noticed that? Someone who, deep down, views himself with contempt treats others with contempt. Of a truth, in the exact way that we view and treat ourselves—we view and treat others.

As we journey on the walk of life it is imperative that we pack the provision called love. We are to embrace God's love for us and love him in return. We are to love our Self, which is the proper response of a grateful heart. We are to love one another.

Grace

Our fourth provision is grace. The basic meaning of our word grace is "an undeserved gift." But this is basic indeed—about as basic as the jar full of Pacific Ocean I talked about earlier.

Once again, I am thankful that we can embrace what we cannot explain, for I cannot explain grace. Tozer has it right: "Grace in its true New Testament meaning is foreign to human reason, not because it is contrary to reason but because it lies beyond it. The doctrine of grace had to be revealed; it could not have been discovered."

But what is grace? It is unearned and undeserved bountiful favor. It is the energizing desire, ability, and resource to do what we are called to do—pursue and experience our psychospiritual growth. Grace runs contrary to the judicial mandate—it gives what is not deserved.

Grace abounds. It is grace that calls us to the walk of life. It is grace that quickens our spirit, instilling life. It is grace that sustains and equips and accompanies our walk. And it is grace, as John Newton tells us, that will lead us home.

As I said, grace abounds. God does not extend grace to us in miserly fashion. That is the human way—to give only as much as is needed, if that. God pours his grace out in superabundance. He "lavishes" it upon us, to use the Apostle Paul's word, dispensing it benevolently.

Just as we must be willing to receive grace we must also be willing to extend it to others. We must willingly give to others what they do not deserve. A kind word, a second or even seventy-second chance, a helping hand, all are acts of grace. When we extend grace to others we show better than any spoken word that although we cannot explain what grace is, we have experienced it. We can give, because we have received.

As you travel the walk of life remember that you are not limited to your own resources. There is an unseen divine assistance which surrounds you and permeates you. This, and so much more, is what grace is all about.

Mercy

Susan and I often tell our children that ours is a home established on grace and mercy. While we live this out imperfectly, it is our desire that our children be solidly assured of these twin realities in our home.

Grace and mercy are related truths. While grace is the giving of that which is undeserved, mercy is the withholding of that which is deserved. Mercy has to do with being longsuffering, forgiving, compassionate. The walk of life is not governed by the judicial mandate, that is, by legalism. Mercy's question is not "How might I punish?" but "How might I righteously refrain from punishing?" The more litigious our society becomes, looking to legal answers as the resolution to our problems, the less mercy we see. Thank God that he does not deal with us on the basis of the judicial mandate (the transgression of his laws) but on the basis of his mercy.

Unmerciful people are inherently cruel. How unlike God this is. They are blind in their shadowy, unconscious living—oblivious to the mercy God has extended to them.

God deals with us, and we therefore deal with one another in one of two fashions. In every situation, in every instance, we either apply justice or we apply mercy. Listen to what C. S. Lewis tells us:

> The essential act of mercy was to pardon; and pardon in its very essence involves the recognition of guilt and ill-desert in the recipient. If crime is only a disease which needs cure, not sin which deserves punishment, it cannot be pardoned. How can you pardon a man for having a gumboil or a club foot? But the Humanitarian theory wants simply to abolish Justice and substitute Mercy for it. This means that you start being "kind" to people before you have considered their rights, and then force upon them supposed kindnesses which no one but you will recognize as kindnesses and which the recipient will feel as abominable cruelties. You have overshot the mark. Mercy, detached from Justice, grows unmerciful. That is the important paradox. As there are plants which will flourish only in mountain soil, so it appears that Mercy will flower only when it grows in the crannies of the rock Justice: transplanted to the marshlands of mere Humanitarianism, it becomes a man-eating weed, all the

more dangerous because it is still called by the same name as the mountain variety.[1]

God, in his infinite goodness had ten thousands times rather extend his mercy than his justice to us. But it will be either this or that. He must be true to his perfect nature. We, on the other hand, had rather extend justice than mercy. Or at least it is our unconscious initial reaction to do so. If you doubt this, think of your initial response the last time someone cut you off in traffic, or the last time a bank teller treated you rudely, or the last time your child broke a vase.

We bristle at the concept of God's justice but the fact of the matter is that we are a million times more justice-based in our thinking than God is. It is we who are the legalists, the judicially focused beings (except of course, when we are the guilty party), not God. He is merciful.

King David understood perfectly this dark insight into human nature. David had willfully disobeyed God. The Lord sent a prophet to David saying "This is what the LORD says: I am giving you three options. Choose one of them for me to carry out against you." In brief, the three choices were of two distinct types. Either God would directly judge David for his sin or he would allow David to fall into the hands of his enemies for a short period of time. David's response? "Let me fall into the hands of the LORD, for his mercy is very great; *but do not let me fall into the hands of men.*"[2] (emphasis added) The king understood full well this distinction between the nature of God and the nature of man. God prefers mercy. Man prefers judgment.

"It is of the LORD's mercies that we are not consumed [that is, do not receive justice]" says Jeremiah, "because his compassions fail not. They are new every morning." While

---

[1] C. S. Lewis, *God in the Dock* (William B. Eerdmans Publishing Company, 1970), 294.

[2] 1 Chron. 21:13.

we humans prepare an ongoing record of grievances committed against us, longing for judicial reckoning, God begins every day afresh—with new mercies and new compassions for us.

If you are one of the many who has been wounded by the judicial zealotry of unmerciful parenting or organized religion chalk it up to the depravity of the human heart—but not to God. It is not his preferred mode. He is the extender of "tender mercies," as David says over and over in the Psalms.

As you travel your walk, do not be driven by perfectionism, do not flagellate yourself for your failures and shortcomings. Our God is a God of mercy. Only when we understand and experience this will we begin to extend mercy to others.

Peace

The last of the provisions which we will consider is now before us. It is the provision of peace. Americans consume more than two tons—two tons, mind you—of Valium per day. Anxiety and the stress it generates is one of the greatest killers in our society. We are a people sorely in need of peace.

Peace is never achieved by pursuing peace. It is a by-product, a fruit of psychospiritual development. It is a grace-gift from the Prince of Peace.

Peace is the evidence that our God-created Self is in harmony with what it is supposed to be. This is why anxiety could be a useful tool if we would allow it to—and would listen to it. Anxiety is the psyche's way of telling us that we are out of whack. That something is wrong. Anxiety is a call to correction.

As we travel the walk of life there is no need to hurry, no need to panic. (Like the inexperienced hiker, the initiate to the walk of life typically starts out at a frenetic pace.) It is not as though we have to be at a certain stage of development by a certain time. Relax. God does not want us just to arrive, he wants us to enjoy the trip.

I want to share something with you which is very dear to my heart. My maternal grandmother and I were very, very close. She was my friend and spiritual mentor. She died last year at the age of one hundred and two. My friend and grandmother was born in 1890 and began the walk of life in 1905. She traveled on for eighty-seven years after that—and no doubt, still travels on today. She was the greatest living example of peace I have ever known. Life did not eat at her the way it so often does me. She somehow transcended the hardships and difficulties, the anxieties that came her way. She was centered.

Not long before my grandmother died she and I sat together talking. I asked her about this very thing. "Mom, how is it," I asked, "that life doesn't eat you up the way it sometimes does me? You just seem to know how to live." She looked at me and said calmly (she was always calm), "Well, it's just about love. You have to love the Lord." That, she said, was the secret to her peace. I hope that the next time I see her I can say to her "Mom, I finally got it."

We have looked at six essential provisions for the walk of life: faith, hope, love, grace, mercy, and peace. There are more. But these are a start—and they are essential. In our closing chapter I would like to recommend to you, my fellow-traveler, four prayers.

God made no tools for himself, he needs none; he created himself a partner in the dialogue of time, and one who is capable of holding converse with him.[1]

—Martin Buber

CHAPTER 14

Prayers for the Road

I want to open with a word of candor and confession regarding our subject. I have always struggled with prayer. Certain contents in my own shadow cause me to automatically believe that there is no way God is interested in listening to me. I have to do battle with this constantly. I can teach, or study, or write, or do therapy for hours. But prayer is hard for me. I could do much better at it if I could simply get out of my own mind and just *do it*. But this does not come naturally for me. I seem forever to get off in my own thought life and forget that I am talking to and listening to somebody (as God's Spirit attempts to speak to my heart and mind).

Having made this admission, I want to proceed by suggesting four prayers which I believe to be essential if we are to successfully confront our shadow and travel the walk of life. Regularly and persistently we must pray for honesty, courage, consciousness, and illumination.

Honesty

We should pray for honesty. When the ancients prayed they often did so with their palms facing upward and their

[1] Martin Buber, *The Writings of Martin Buber*, ed. Will Herberg (Meridian Books, 1956), 270.

hands open. While there is certainly no divinely-prescribed prayer posture I would suggest that you practice this from time to time. It is a physical metaphor. It is a way of saying to God—and reinforcing in our mind—that we are coming to him with no hidden agenda, no duplicity. We are coming before him open and honest.[1]

I love to hear beginners on the walk of life pray. They pray with such childlike honesty. They simply talk to God. If they join a church it is usually not long, sadly, until this has changed altogether. The clichés, the rote expressions heard in prayer in every church I have ever known soon show up in their prayers.[2] We are going to talk about praying *for* honesty but it is at least equally important that we pray *in* honesty.

Our shadow is reminiscent of our archetypal parents in the garden. When the heat is on, it longs to head for the bushes. We need to pray that we would respond in honesty when the truth shines upon our shadow like some great light. Light responded to brings greater light. Light rejected intensifies the darkness.

An often painful honesty is required to confront the shadow. Each of us has that part of self we would prefer to neither see nor know. Listen to how John Sanford addresses this: ". . . psychological honesty, that is, the development of the capacity to be honest with oneself about oneself [is required]. This kind of honesty is the *sine qua non* of spiritual and psychological development."[3] Woven into the texture

---

[1] One of the greatest benefits of this little practice is that it is a terrific exercise for combating the shadow, which in no way likes being out in the open. Try it and you will see (feel) what I mean.

[2] A pastor-friend of mine told me the story of how one Sunday morning the ushers came forward to collect the offering. The pastor asked one of the ushers to pray. The usher's mental Rolodex pulled up the standard church meal prayer instead of the standard offertory prayer. As he stood there with the collection plate in his hand he prayed: "Lord, we thank you for this food and pray that you will bless it to the nourishment of our bodies." It brought down the house!

[3] John A. Sanford, *The Strange Trial of Mr. Hyde*, 151.

of the fall is a patently dishonest spirit which, I believe, is the result of a pervasive sense of deficiency. This inner dishonesty is the most primal reaction to the consciousness that something is deeply wrong inside. Think again of the garden. Adam and Eve's complete energy suddenly went into covering their own tail. Hear what Jung says about this:

> The shadow is a moral problem that challenges the whole ego-personality, for no one can become conscious of the shadow without considerable moral effort. To become conscious of it involves recognizing the dark aspects of the personality as present and real. This act is the essential condition for any kind of self-knowledge, and it therefore, as a rule, meets with considerable resistance.[1]

We must recognize that the dark aspects of the personality are present and real. This does not mean a general, amorphous assent to admitting that I am a "sinner." The world is full of people who will assent to being sinners in general but not to their own shadow in particular. This is why we must pray for honesty.

This honesty is essential to real self-knowledge. Imagine having a musty old trunk in your attic marked "My Shadow." You are about to open that trunk to discover and examine its contents. The prayer for honesty says "I am willing to see whatever is there, and to take it for what it is." This is scary. It is often painful. But as painful as it is, without this kind of integrity of spirit, we will simply go on in unconsciousness and shadowy self-delusion.

And be ready, for your shadow will resist this kind of honesty, just as Jung says. But without this integrity of spirit, there will be no individuation, no psychospiritual growth.

Like individuation or spiritual growth itself, this kind of honesty is a process. We are not talking in absolute terms here, that is: "Yes, I am honest with and about myself," or

---

[1] C. G. Jung, *The Portable Jung* (The Viking Press, 1971), 145.

"No, I am not honest with and about myself." Personality is not that static. The goal is to grow in honesty as we grow in consciousness. Indeed, you cannot do the one without the other.

Remember, the honesty I am referring to is honesty with self. This is the honesty we must pray for because it is primary. No one will ever be honest with God or anyone else until he is first honest with himself about himself. Honesty with oneself is the bedrock of psychospiritual health. There is very little in psychological and spiritual pathology which cannot be dealt with if the individual will just admit its existence.

When I am honest with others about myself, even God, I am practicing what I call communicated honesty. But when I am honest with myself about my shadow I am practicing primary honesty. This is where it all begins. For example, I have a colleague who will from time to time tell his clients: "I am not so much concerned that you are lying to me in therapy. I am not primarily concerned that you are lying to your wife. But I am greatly distressed that you are lying to yourself."

The intrinsically dishonest individual does not pray because she does not want to see the truth about herself. This is why Adam and Eve hid from God, and why we do too. All but the insipidly stupid—or the totally depraved—know that they cannot con God with a bogus presentation of self. We *know* that God knows. We avoid prayer because *we* do not wish to know. This is why we must pray for honesty.

There is a great danger to intrinsic dishonesty. We can practice this for so long that we become entirely self-deluded. It is possible to actually deteriorate psychospiritually to the point that you are convinced that you have no shadow. Think of the Pharisee's prayer: "Oh God, I thank you that I am not like other people . . . ." Now, this man was no unlearned fool. He was a theologian. He knew that one cannot con God. He knew that God *knows*. But he had practiced primary dishonesty for so long that he was totally self-deluded. He had worn the religious mask so long it had finally become the face itself. I am convinced that he absolutely believed what he was praying. Our Lord himself said that there was no hope for this individual as long as he continued to practice such self-deluding primary dishonesty. Poor man.

Courage

We must pray for courage. We will never be honest with ourselves without courage—we will never see the need for courage if we are not honest with ourselves. Opening that trunk which I spoke about above is scary work. We have spent a good portion of our life's energy packing things away there and getting that trunk as far away from our day to day life as possible.

Why do we need to pray for courage? Because without the heart for change there is no hope of growth. The heart for change is such an important factor in life that it— the ability to constructively deal with change—is actually one of the determinants of mental health. Why? Because one cannot grow beyond her boundaries. And growth shatters all previous forms. This is why we pray for courage—change requires it.

We pray for courage because facing the shadow is a painful process. Jolande Jacobi, a student and colleague of Jung tells us, "To confront the shadow thus means to take a mercilessly critical attitude toward one's own nature."[1] This is exactly why I said in chapter twelve that the self-absorbed do not pursue psychospiritual growth. Their filtering question is "How does this make me feel?" Very often facing the

---

[1] Jolande Jacobi, *The Psychology of C. G. Jung*, (Yale University Press, 1973), 109-110.

shadow makes one feel miserable. They will not take that mercilessly critical attitude toward their own nature that Jacobi speaks of. It does not feel good. This is why, after disclosing his struggle with his own shadow, the Apostle Paul cried out, "O wretched man that I am."

Jung believed that every "awakened Christian"—his term—has the same serious psychic experience as that of the Apostle Paul, the experience of confronting his or her own shadow.

Confrontation of the shadow is the personal Calvary which each seeker on the walk of life must face. This is the only way the God-created Self is freed from the shadow and the egocentric ego. Jung equated confronting the shadow with a kind of suffering. He says, ". . . the realization of the shadow [which is] the growing awareness of the inferior part of the personality . . . has . . . the meaning of a suffering and a passion that implicate the whole man."[1] It is inevitable. It is inevitable and it is difficult. So we pray for courage.

Consciousness

Along with honesty and courage we must pray for consciousness. "The greatest of faults," wrote Thomas Carlyle, "is to be conscious of none." Tozer puts it this way, "Of all forms of deception self-deception is the most deadly, and of all deceived persons the self-deceived are the least likely to discover the fraud." Both Carlyle and Tozer are correct and this is why we must pray for consciousness.

Much about the work of therapy has to do with the generation of insight—of bringing unconsciousness into consciousness. Time and time again the therapist will here the client say "I never knew that I was like that," or "I never dreamed I was doing that to her," or such like. And of course this is usually true. Most of the day-to-day harm done in

---

[1] C. G. Jung, *The Collected Works of C. G. Jung*, vol. 8, *The Structure and Dynamics of the Psyche*, 208.

this world occurs not because of a willful intent to harm but because of lazy, unconscious living. To be conscious is to be aware. It is to go through life awake and not asleep. Do not make the mistake of thinking that being religious is the same thing as being spiritually conscious. Previously we discussed the life of Paul before his conversion to the Way. He persecuted those who were on the walk of life. Now, Paul was a religious man—devoutly, even zealously so—but he did not have a clue. Listen to his own honest self-revelation about his unconscious living:

> I'm so grateful to Christ Jesus for making me adequate to do this work. He went out on a limb, you know, in trusting me with this ministry. The only credentials I brought to it were invective and witch hunts and arrogance. But I was treated mercifully because I didn't know what I was doing—didn't know who I was doing it against! Grace mixed with faith and love poured over me and into me.[1]

This is why one cannot equate religion with spirituality. Paul had religion—lots of it. But he was not spiritually alive, spiritually conscious. Religion and spirituality are not the same at all, anymore than a hospital is the same thing as sound health.

Society is largely ignorant. This is true because the constituent members of society are by and large ignorant. Before dismissing me as an egotist, please hear me out. Though the word is used in all sorts of ways the basic meaning of ignorance is "not knowing." That is, not being conscious of something. It comes from the same root as "ignore." We have taken the word and narrowed it to little more than an aca-

---

[1] 1 Tim. 1:12-14, *THE MESSAGE.* This is similar to the Laodecian church spoken of in the third chapter of the New Testament book of the Revelation. They were so very proud of their condition. They considered themselves to be quite spiritual, but Christ pronounced them to be spiritually "poor, blind, and naked." They were unconscious of their actual state.

demic meaning—like this: ignorance = uneducated. But there are a great number of people who lack formal education who are by no means ignorant. They do not live unconsciously. Conversely, there are a good number of people who could hardly be called uneducated but who are ignorant because they chose to live unconsciously—to live in the Shadowlands.

I earlier referred to the Johnson administration and the Vietnam war. I do so again to illustrate my point. Johnson's advisors could hardly be called an uneducated lot. They were the Ivy League's finest—the "best and the brightest." But I submit that in terms of the Vietnam mess they acted in sheer ignorance. Unconscious, shadowy dynamics ruled the decision making in much of that whole sad debacle.

To individuate, to experience psychospiritual growth, is to increasingly cultivate conscious living. Consciousness is not an achievement but an evolution. This brings up an interesting point.

I believe consciousness is a grace-gift. What I mean is this. I believe that in his mercy, God will not give us more consciousness than we are able to bear, than is good and needful for us at any given stage of growth. If absolute consciousness were available I would not want it. I could not handle it. In his mercy, God will not overload us with consciousness. He will not give us more than we can stand. We do not have to worry about this. Our problem lies in the other direction.

Perhaps the first consciousness we stand in need of is that of realizing our calling to live as an individual before God—to be true to our God-created Self. Recall from earlier that this is similar to that which Kierkegaard suggests: "the consciousness before God of one's eternal responsibility to be an individual is that one thing necessary."[1]

---

[1] Søren Kierkegaard, *Purity of Heart is to Will One Thing*, 197-198.

Following hard after this call to live as an individual is the call to begin the walk of life, to commit ourselves to our psychospiritual development. If we are uninterested in the spiritual life it is not because we lack the need but because we lack the consciousness of that need. A good prayer for the individual who is at that point in life might be "God, if there is anything to this, I ask you to make me conscious of that need within me."

After this follows the day-to-day consciousness we need to progress in our walk, the consciousness we need—when we need it—to experience ever more the God-created Self we were called to be. This is the consciousness we pray for.

Illumination

The last prayer I would like to suggest is the prayer for illumination. Illumination is the urgent need of the hour. Illumination is difficult to define because of the mystical nature of it. Nevertheless, it is something that through the centuries those on the walk of life have earnestly sought and honored.

Illumination is a greater and deeper experience of consciousness. Illumination is exclusively the *quickening*, to use the good old word, work of God's Spirit in our mind and spirit. Illumination is that wonderfully mysterious occurrence that gives life to consciousness. Consciousness makes us aware; illumination breathes life into the conscious facts.

Have you ever thought about how many of the miracles Christ performed had to do with restoring sight to the blind? These were miracles of metaphor. Think about how often Christ talked about eyes and seeing.

For example, when the religious leaders of the day showed little tolerance and understanding of spiritual truth he called them the "blind leaders of the blind," and "blind guides." When his own most intimate followers, the twelve, were ignorant of a particular truth he was trying to teach them, Christ said "Having eyes, do you not see?"

Illumination is having our spiritual eyes opened. It has to do with the giving (from the Spirit of God) and the receiving (in our mind and spirit) of spiritual truth. This is precisely what the Apostle Paul means when he tells us:

> The unspiritual self, just as it is by nature, can't receive the gifts of God's Spirit. There's no capacity for them. They seem like so much silliness. Spirit can be known only by spirit—God's Spirit and our spirits in open communion. Spiritually alive, we have access to everything God's Spirit is doing, and can't be judged by unspiritual critics.
>
> Isaiah's question, "Is there anyone around who knows God's Spirit, anyone who knows what he is doing?" has been answered: Christ knows, and we have Christ's Spirit.[1]

Jesus himself referred to this same subject. He told those who had newly committed to the walk of life, "I still have many things to tell you, but you can't handle them now. But when the Friend comes, the Spirit of the Truth, he will take you by the hand and guide you into all the truth there is." This is why spiritual seekers through the millennia have prayed the simple prayer "Open Thou my eyes."

We have in the Apostle Peter a superb example of illumination at work. Here is the account:

> When Jesus came to the region of Caesarea Philippi, he asked his disciples, "Who do people say the Son of Man is?"
>
> They replied, "Some say John the Baptist; others say Elijah; and still others, Jeremiah or one of the prophets."
>
> "But what about you?" he asked. "Who do you say I am?"

---

[1] 1 Cor. 2:14-16, *THE MESSAGE.*

Simon Peter answered, "You are the Christ, the Son of the living God."

Jesus replied, "Blessed are you, Simon son of Jonah, for this was not revealed to you by man, but by my Father in heaven."[1]

That is illumination.

We need to have our minds illumined to the greater reality of the spiritual world. The person who has committed to her psychospiritual growth creates nothing by her faith. She is merely getting in touch with what is. The spiritual world is *invisible* but it is not *imaginary*. There is all the difference in the world between these two terms.

Listen once again to the spiritual guide, A. W. Tozer:

> Our trouble is that we have established bad thought habits. We habitually think of the visible world as real and doubt the reality of any other. We do not deny the existence of the spiritual world but we doubt that it is real in the accepted meaning of the word.
>
> The world of sense intrudes upon our attention day and night for the whole of our lifetime. It is clamorous, insistent and self-demonstrating. It does not appeal to our faith; it is here, assaulting our five senses, demanding to be accepted as real and final. . . .
>
> Our uncorrected thinking, influenced by the blindness of our natural hearts and the intrusive ubiquity of visible things, tends to draw a contrast between the spiritual and the real; but actually no such contrast exists. The antithesis lies elsewhere: between the real and the imaginary, between the spiritual and the material, between the temporal and the eternal; but between the spiritual and the real, never. The spiritual *is* real. . . .
>
> But we must avoid the common fault of pushing the "other world" into the future. It is not future, but present.

---

[1] Mt. 16:13-17.

It parallels our familiar physical world, and the doors between the two worlds are open.[1]

Spiritual illumination is urgently needed. This is as true for the church as it is for you and me as individuals. Without illumination the truth entrusted to the church becomes nothing more than theological data, no different than, say, a textbook on electrical engineering. The result is dead orthodoxy. And dead orthodoxy never gives nor sustains life. In fact, it kills. I have no doubt whatsoever that this is precisely why many who are genuinely seeking the spiritual life are leaving the church in record numbers.

While we cannot generate illumination—remember, it comes from the Spirit of God to our spirit—we can prepare the ground for the good seed. Prayer, meditation on scripture and other truths, reading the classics and the modern authors who write of the walk of life, taking time for reflection in solitude, interacting with others in redemptive community all can be useful to this end. This all takes discipline and time—which is bad news to a people living at such a pace that we are traveling faster than the speed of life. We have become slaves to the tyranny of the urgent.

Some of the greatest moments I ever experience in therapy, and this is true for my clients as well, is when illumination descends—I know of no better way to put it—on the session. It is a mystical, wonderful encounter. It is as though truth suddenly settles upon us. It is as though at that very instant great blinders have been lifted from our spiritual eyes and we *see*. In therapy as in ordinary life, when such times of illumination occur it is like we take a quantum leap in our growth. "A moment's insight is sometimes worth a life's experience," said Oliver Wendell Holmes. This is what happens when the Spirit illumines our spirit with truth.

---

[1] A. W. Tozer, *The Pursuit of God*, 56-58.

I would like to give a personal example of illumination which came to me as I was working on this book. I had a good week of writing and was thinking about this as I stepped into the whirlpool. I started to offer up a prayer of thanksgiving for the good week as I entered the soothing hot water. Immediately I felt unworthy to do this (remember my admission at the outset of this chapter), and hesitated for a brief moment. Instantly my mind was illumined with this idea and I have no doubt that it was a word from God's Spirit to my own: "That's okay. Disregard that you *feel* unworthy and thank God anyway, as though you *are* worthy." I did so.

Now, I *knew* this, of course. It is pretty basic theology. But my knowledge had slipped to being nothing more than cold cognizance of the fact. The *spirit* of this truth—the life and energy of it—had slipped away from me. Interestingly, though this is hardly significant to the facts, I began to feel differently about the matter as well. Now, this was no cognitive or behavioral psychology trick but a spiritual truth which illumined my mind at that moment. I mean, I am on the walk of life, I am pursuing growth and wholeness. Of course God is delighted to hear my prayer of thankfulness to him.

One final word about illumination. When illumination comes our way, the obvious accompanying reality is that up to that point, we were in darkness (unconsciousness) regarding the content of the particular illumination. The very definition of the word, indeed, the very word itself demands a previous condition of darkness. (You can't "light up" light, only darkness.) If we were in darkness about that truth, how much more is there that we are unconscious of, that we will never know until we are illumined? This should have two immediate effects.

First, it should strike a blow to our hubris and humble us. However much we may know and have experienced, however far we may be down the walk of life, we have no idea how much more, infinitely more there is that we are not conscious of. Second, this fact should infuse us with vigor for the walk of life. As God illumines our spirit, it is as though we are walking along the beach collecting diamonds as the waves wash them ashore! Who knows what, in his bountiful goodness, he may illumine us to next as we travel the walk of life!

CONCLUSION

Our greatest dignity comes in the fact that we are called to embrace and experience our God-created Self and to move ever onward toward psychospiritual wholeness. Not to answer the call to the walk of life leaves but one other option—to stay childish, undeveloped. This is why, given a normal childhood, kids are happy and carefree. They have a small, unconscious world. This is normal for children but not for adults.

The walk of life is the race we are called to run. After describing great men and women who completed their own walk of life, the author of the epistle to the Hebrews says to you and me: "Therefore, since we are surrounded by such a great cloud of witnesses . . . let us run with perseverance the race marked out for us." When we travel the walk of life we join with that vast horde which has gone before—and with those who will come behind us. It is exhilarating to be a part of something so much bigger than yourself!

I am constantly reminding myself and others that life is a marathon, not a 100-meter dash. Take the time to watch the two races sometime and note the differences. The dash is more like the firing of a projectile. It is utter adrenalin and sinew—ten seconds of all-out effort. The walk of life is nothing like this. How many people have I seen get a white-hot intensity for spiritual development, displaying a fervor so great that we were astonished at their focus. And they were focused—for about ten seconds.

No, the walk of life is not like that. It is not a dash but a marathon. In distance running the rules are different. Pacing, rhythm are required. You know a long climb lies just ahead. You pace yourself. You have to pick your times, though still running, to rest yourself. Distance runners are not frantic. They glide. Notice them sometime. Rhythm is crucial because all excess thrashing burns, wastes the precious energy needed to carry on.

Although I never ran a marathon, I used to run seven to ten miles a day, six days a week (a practice since given up for walking). Building up to this distance I noticed the improvement in my stride, my rhythm. I can still recall how I enjoyed running through the quiet of the wooded trails hearing just the slightest rhythmic sound as over and over my feet made contact with the ground. I would think on how my stride had changed from my beginnings, when I was enduring a one-half mile run. Comparatively, I sounded like a stampeding yak back then! Now, and runners will understand this, I felt as if I could run forever. It's all about stamina and endurance, pace and rhythm.

A final illustrative point. Like distance running, the walk of life is hard. That's just the nature of the thing—the nature of the true good life. Watching a marathon on TV one day I noticed something quite remarkable. The cameras were on the finish line and the place was packed with anxious fans. (The race, as marathons sometimes do, ended in a stadium.) As the winner crossed the line I was startled. The guy had an erect, high, bouncy, almost *prancing* stride. His shirt was neatly tucked in. He was not even sweating. In fact, he was smiling from ear to ear waving at the camera. I had never seen anything like this in a distance race. I had never finished ten miles looking like that, let alone twenty-six! A minute or so later other runners started to stagger in looking as haggard as distance runners should.

Shortly the mystery was solved. This man had jumped onto the course just outside the stadium. He was well prepared. He even had a bogus number pinned to his shirt. This was nothing more than a joke performed by the class clown—a stunt for camera and crowd. He was not in the race at all.

As you travel the walk of life do not worry that someone may be passing you or that you are not as fast as others. You are measured only against yourself—where you are, in relation to where you were. So just walk on. Concentrate on pacing yourself. Watch your rhythm. The race is not to the swift. The walk of life is not a dash. And remember while you press on, you are not there by yourself. We are in the arena, but we are not alone.

Dr. Mike Ruth
PO Box 32805
Knoxville, TN 37930-2805

DrMikeRuth@aol.com

We need not deny that modern doubt, like ancient doubt, does ask deep questions; we only deny that, as compared with our own philosophy, it gives any deeper answers. And it is a general rule, touching what is called modern thought, that while the questions are often really deep, the answers are often decidedly shallow. And it is even perhaps more important to remark that, while the questions are in a sense eternal, the answers are in every sense ephemeral. . . . Those who leave the tradition of truth do not escape into something which we call Freedom. They only escape into something else, which we call Fashion.[1]

—G. K. Chesterton

APPENDIX

Understanding the Church

Earlier this century a prominent family-owned British newspaper obtained a new editor-in-chief. The patriarch of the paper, a man of much renown and respect in London had retired and his son was now at the helm. Under his leadership changes were made that were not at all popular with many of the older readers. While walking to his office one day the new editor was accosted on the street by an elderly lady who proceeded to chide him for "ruining" the paper. She declared to the startled young man that the paper was no longer as good as it used to be. Calmly—and wisely—the new editor replied, "Madam, it never has been."

The same type of nostalgic romanticism is found today among Christians regarding the quality of the church today, as compared to previous generations. A common misconception today is that while the modern church is lacking

---

[1] G. K. Chesterton, in *The Outline of Sanity* by Alzina Stone Dale (Eerdmans Publishing Company, 1982), 268.

in both spiritual power and influence, the "Church of our Fathers" was a bulwark of spiritual might. This opinion does not jibe with reality, as any student of church history knows. To paraphrase the young editor, the church was never as good in the past as later generations deemed it. This is true even of the very earliest of churches. The New Testament church at Corinth was a zoo. In the same era, the church at Ephesus was strongly divided along socioeconomic lines and was given to not a little materialism.

The fact remains however, that there are some serious problems. I recall attending a lecture with the late theologian Francis Schaeffer, in which he stated that there are three conditions in our society which have never before existed. According to Dr. Schaeffer, there has never been a time when so many people claim to be born again, there have never been so many people attending Evangelical churches, and there has never been a time when the church has had so little impact. Just what is wrong with the church?

Recently a friend and I were talking about the state of things. She became somewhat defensive, feeling I was being too harsh in my assessment. At one point she remarked sarcastically "Oh, I know. The church is such an easy target for people who want to be critical." She went on in her defense of the church to add that there are no more problems here than there are in any other organization.

But there is a gaping hole in my friend's reasoning. And what she stated was exactly the point I was attempting to make. The church is (and should be) judged more harshly because of what it purports to be and because of the claims it makes. Let me explain.

Suppose the local cable television company is known to employ several gossips, a philanderer or two, and a majority of people who take no interest whatsoever in their own psychospiritual growth, let alone that of their customers. The residents may think this a sad thing, may regret that such is the case, and may even ridicule the company for having such a sordid host of people working there.

But I doubt it. What the cable customers are looking for from the company is prompt and reliable service, polite workers, and a good rate. Period. The consumers are not looking for the employees of that business to explain to them the meaning of life nor to show them how to live. It might be preferable if the company employs such exemplary people—even desirable. But it is not essential. The fact of the matter is that cable TV companies do not exist to answer the existential questions of life.

Take another example. The local country club may be comprised largely of the stereotypically arrogant, small-souled egotists that are rightly or wrongly associated with these organizations. However, if the golf course is a fine championship-rated masterpiece, then one will likely hold his nose and play through.

Why? Because one joins the country club to play golf, not to find truth. He may be looking for someone who can help lower his handicap but in all probability he did not join the club to secure a spiritual guide.

Why the Church is Different

Now consider the church. If one thinks about it, the claims made by the church—and the pronouncements Christ makes regarding the church—are positively staggering.

The church is the only institution on earth to be founded by Jesus Christ. As crucial to life as they are, Jesus did not organize a single hospital. Orphanages, relief efforts for those in need, homes and hospices for the aged, facilities for the incurably ill, as important as all of these are, none can claim to have Jesus Christ as its founder. Yet our Lord said "I will build my church." Note the possessive—*my* church, Jesus says. Further, it is quite one thing to bring a project into being, another altogether to provide for its maintenance and continuation. In this same verse Jesus declares and promises that hell itself will be unable to prevail against the church. Not only did he found the church, Jesus also guarantees its continued existence.

The Lord sometimes has a funny way of illustrating his point. The eighteenth-century French philosopher Voltaire was an avid antichrist. At least he was consistent—he loathed the church as well. He boasted that the force and influence of his writings would be such as to reduce Christianity to rubble. He wrote extensively to that end, fueled by his hatred for Jesus and his church. Things did not quite turn out as Voltaire had planned, however. Shortly after his death, Voltaire's house was purchased by a Bible society as a storage warehouse for Bibles they planned to distribute!

Jesus has not only established the church, he has also decreed its endurance—its permanence. He has declared "I will build my church." And so he has. He has proclaimed "and the gates of hell will not prevail against it." And so they have not.

We must realize exactly what it is the church professes to be. Then one can easily see why it is judged by a different standard, why my friend was so terribly off base with her attempt to defend the church by stating that "the church is no worse off than any other organization."

The tremendous heritage of the church is encapsulated in three Biblical metaphors, one primary and two secondary. That is to say, the two spring forth from the one.

The Church as Citadel of Truth

The primary metaphor is introduced by St. Paul, in his First Epistle to Timothy.[1] In a passage discussing various practices to be observed by local congregations, Paul refers

---

[1] 1 Tim 3:15.

to the church as "the pillar and foundation of the truth." Do we really understand what an audacious statement this is?

Paul is essentially saying that the very foundational principles—the bedrock—one needs for life are given to us in the truth revealed to and through the church. He is saying that the church is to be the citadel of truth.

This past summer my family and I visited historic Williamsburg, Virginia. Being a former history teacher and lover of the subject, I was delighted with the place. Located somewhat centrally in that graceful old town is the munitions magazine. This is where the rifles and sidearms, along with whatever artillery the capital of the Virginia colony possessed, were kept. The powder and shot for these weapons were kept there as well. Should a skirmish or battle arise, the local militia would rush to the magazine for their munitions.

This simple illustration clarifies for us what Paul is saying in 1 Timothy 3:15. He is telling us that the basic weapons, the tools which we need to fight our spiritual battles have been placed for safekeeping in the church. It is there, in the repository of revealed truth, that one will secure what is necessary to develop the potentials of life and where one will be equipped to fight life's spiritual battles.

My graduate studies on both the master's and doctoral levels have concentrated in the arena of psychology while incorporating theological studies. In all of my training and experience in the counseling arena as well as my years in the pastorate, I have yet to encounter any sound psychological principles that contradict the basic truths about living that are given in the Bible. To be sure, they expand upon the nascent truths given there. This is not surprising as the Bible does not attempt to be a manual in psychology. However, good psychology and good Biblical hermeneutics are never at odds. They are complimentary.[1] I often present this truth to my clients this way, "It is impossible for me to believe that something can be good for me spiritually but be bad for me psychologically. Likewise, I cannot believe something makes good psychological sense for me but will harm my spiritual life." Good psychology and sound theology are co-laborers together for our psychospiritual growth and development. This is why I prefer and use the term *psychospiritual*. An awkward term, perhaps—but the accurate one nonetheless.

Recall that I have said there is one primary and two secondary Biblical metaphors which demonstrate why the church is accountable to higher standards of scrutiny than are organizations of purely human origins. We have just taken a brief look at the primary metaphor, the church as the pillar and foundation of the truth. It is now time to consider the secondary metaphors, which are presented as a couplet by Jesus. They are disclosed in the fifth chapter of the Gospel of Matthew.[2]

The Church as Salt

The first of the secondary metaphors is presented in verse thirteen. There, Jesus declares to his followers that they are the "salt of the earth." This notion is replete with wonderful applications.

I recall as a child hearing my father tell the story of how, when he was a lad, he cut his hand with an ax while chopping kindling for his momma's cook stove. He rushed into the house and immediately after rinsing the gash with water, my grandmother packed the wound with salt. In those

---

[1] Indeed, for me, there is a beautiful complementarianism between the two. The essential focus of theology is *content*; the essential focus of psychology and psychotherapy is *process*. The synergy is exquisite.

[2] Chapters 5, 6, and 7 of Matthew's Gospel comprise that wonderfully pedagogical passage of scripture known as the Sermon on the Mount.

days salt was used medicinally as a healing agent and as a barrier against infection. To this day my father can recall the immediate and furious onset of burning caused by the salt. But he can also remember that there was no subsequent infection, and that his hand soon healed.

The truth which has been entrusted to the church is to be a kind of salt which offers a healing balm for the psychospiritual wounds we experience as we proceed through life. What we seem to dislike most is the fact that the healing brought about by the salt of truth hurts in much the same way that the salt poured in to my father's open wound burned so intensely. The truth will set us free, just as Jesus said—but before it does it will frequently make us miserable.

Very often in psychotherapy I will explain this fact to the client—the fact that the curative, healing work of truth is usually painful. Virtually without exception the individual will declare some variation of "It doesn't matter. I am willing to do whatever it takes to move beyond this." As we reach one of those points in therapy where the process becomes difficult and the client becomes resistant, I will remind him that I warned of the pain involved. Characteristically, the client will usually respond with "Yes, but I didn't know it would be *this* painful!"

There is a sting to the healing power of truth. This is what it means to apply the salt. But having said this we should remember: while God may hurt us, he will never harm us.

But there is more to this metaphor of the church as the salt of the earth. Salt is also a spice, a flavor enhancer. If Thoreau is correct, if the majority of people do lead lives of quiet desperation, then it is the responsibility of those who walk the walk of life to manifest a way of being which shows that we were made for more than this—more than just living a desperate existence only to die a cold death.

I believe this is precisely the point behind our Lord's first miracle which, not so incidently, was performed at a festive occasion—a wedding.[1] Along the way in the celebration (which often lasted several days), the host ran out of wine. This was a most humiliating situation for the host and something that would get him talked about all over the little town of Cana, in the region of Galilee. At his mother's prompting, Jesus instructed the servants at the banquet to fill six large stone pots with water, which they proceeded to do. At this point the miracle occurs as Jesus turned the water to wine. So good was that wine in fact that the guests marveled at the magnanimity of their host for saving the very best drink until last.

Many have puzzled at why Jesus began his earthly ministry with such a seemingly trivial display of his power. I believe they miss the point of the miracle. Nothing is more common than water. Being the most abundant compound on the planet, it covers more than three-fourths of the earth's surface. As important to life as it is, water is pretty ordinary stuff. I believe this is precisely why our Lord performed his first miracle using it.

Just as with water, there is nothing more common, more ordinary than everyday life. Think of how much time we all spend doing the same things over and over again. We go to work, we take the kids to whatever it is they are currently practicing, we buy the groceries, we mow the lawn, we cook dinner, we do the laundry. Over and over again the routine continues. As someone once said, the problem with life is that it is so daily. I believe what Jesus is trying to tell us with this first miracle is that he came to sanctify the ordinary, to—like salt—put some flavor in our lives. This is why he came. And this is one of the tasks he has left the church to carry on.

---

[1] John 2:1-11.

If, in Christ there is to be found life at its fullest as he says, then of a truth it is incumbent upon the church to exhibit such life by being the salt of the earth. Otherwise, we encounter those disturbing words of our Lord, "If the salt has lost its saltiness, . . . it is no longer good for anything except to be thrown out and trampled by men." How barren and bland life seems when we are not seeking to align ourselves with truth, to be the salt of the earth.

The Church as Light

The other dependent or secondary metaphor follows hard after the first in Matthew five. As Jesus continues delivering the Sermon on the Mount and just after he declares his followers to be the salt of the earth, he completes the couplet. He adds, "You are the light of the world."

As a college freshmen I had a physical science professor by the name of Mr. Cloud. (A fitting name for a physical science professor!) I remember a spelunking expedition several of us participated in with Mr. Cloud. After we had hiked, crawled, slid, and fallen our way about a mile into the bowels of the earth we came to a large room in the cave. I will forever remember what came next. As we sat around on the cave floor, Mr. Cloud gave us a brief lecture on light and darkness. He asked if anyone of us had ever experienced total darkness. All replied in the negative. He described it as a darkness that can be felt. Mr. Cloud went on, "When I count to three everyone turn off your helmet light and flashlight." We did as instructed. We were blinded by the darkness, the total darkness. I can recall holding my hand no more than one inch from my eyes yet being unable to see it. Whether the experience was psychological or sensual I do not know but Mr. Cloud was right—the darkness was palpable. It was heavy. It was suffocating.

This is the kind of psychospiritual darkness which envelopes the world. A darkness which, spiritually, has people groping at noontime as though it were midnight. A darkness which causes people to "stagger like drunkards," as Job says.

Jesus pierced this spiritual darkness. He came as the light of the world. He came as one with both the capacity and the willingness to free us from our darkness, and to lead us out of its clutches. And how gracious that God does not pick favorites. The light is there for anyone's taking.[1] The fact that this information has not been widely embraced as good news says something about how we have grown to love the darkness.[2]

As I write these words I am on the deck of a mountain cabin overlooking a lake. I gaze through the stand of oaks and southern pines and can see the setting sun ignite the lake with its piercing radiance. The whole vista is on fire with beauty. Looking on this beautiful spectacle the mind wonders. How can it be that we so appreciate this world's natural light but shrink so predictably, even methodically, from spiritual light?

Our Lord said, "While I am in the world I am the light of the world." Does this mean that in the many centuries since Christ's departure the world has been light-less? If we believe his words the answer is no.

"You are the light of the world," Jesus proclaimed to his followers. This is the last of our three metaphors.

What does it mean to be the light of the world? It means nothing less than to carry on the life of Jesus. This is at once an awesome responsibility and a glorious privilege.

When I was a pastor I would often remind the congregation that our task was not to attempt an impotent imitation of Jesus. Rather, we are to allow the indwelling Christ to be at home within us—to settle down, if you will—and then to

---

[1] See John 1:9.

[2] According to the words of Jesus, there is a natural tendency to prefer darkness to light because of intrinsic evil (Jn 3:19).

live through us. We must allow him to permeate our existence. This is what it means to be the light of the world. To be sure, this is a great mystery. But as we have said, mystery is nothing new to the church—whose very existence is itself a mystery![1]

So then, to be light is to be life—the life we were created to be. The New Testament equates the two declaring, "In [Jesus] was *life* and the *life* was the *light* of men."[2] Further in John's Gospel, Jesus says that to follow him is to have "the light of life" (8:12). Spiritual death is spiritual darkness. To be light-less is to be lifeless.

The question arises, is the church being true to its calling as the light of the world? Corporately and individually, are we who profess Jesus as Lord demonstrating that light and life go hand-in-hand? Can those who have grown weary of the darkness find their way to spiritual life by our light? Sadly, I think the answer is too often, no.

As I have said, the church should be a place where the light of grace can illumine our shadow, imparting the courage and strength necessary to confront the shadow in a redemptive context. When the church returns to being just such a place, the end result will be personal and corporate growth. And I am convinced that when this occurs Jung will be proven right in his bold statement that, "People may have to go back to the church when they reach a certain stage of analysis,"[3] to complete the education of the soul, to move ever closer to the ultimate goal of individuation or wholeness.

---

[1] Paul informs us that God has disclosed to believers the "glorious riches of this mystery, which is Christ in you, the hope of glory" (Col 1:27). See also Ephesians 5:32.

[2] John 1:4.

[3] C. G. Jung, *C. G. Jung Speaking*, 440.

Dr. Ruth is available for seminars, conferences, human resources consultation (businesses and corporations), and other speaking and consulting needs. For information or scheduling contact:

Dr. Michael Ruth
10005 Lechmeres Point
Knoxville, TN 37922
or e-mail: DrMikeRuth@aol.com

Selected Bibliography

Auden, W. H. *Collected Poems*. New York: Vintage Books, 1991.

Bly, Robert. *The Long Bad We Drag Behind Us*, in *Meeting the Shadow*, eds. Connie Zweig and Jeremiah Abrams. New York: Jeremy P. Tarcher, 1991.

Bonhoeffer, Dietrich. *Life Together*. New York: Harper & Row, 1954.

Buber, Martin. *The Writings of Martin Buber*, ed. Will Herberg. New York: Meridian Books, 1956.

Dale, Alzina Stone. *The Outline of Sanity*. Grand Rapids: Wm. B. Eerdmans Publishing Co., 1982.

Goode, Erica. *Spiritual Questing. U.S. News & World Report*, Dec 7, 1992.

Hanh, Thich Nhat. *Living Buddha, Living Christ*. New York: Riverhead Books, 1995.

Hirsch, Foster. *Love, Sex, Death, and the Meaning of Life*. New York: McGraw-Hill, 1981.

International Bible Society. *The Holy Bible, New International Version*. New York: International Bible Society, 1984.

Jacobi, Jolande. *The Psychology of C. G. Jung*. Translated by Ralph Manheim. New Haven: Yale University Press, 1973.

Jacobsen, Wayne. *The Naked Church*. Eugene: Harvest House Publishers, 1987.

Jung, C. G. *C. G. Jung Speaking*. Edited by William McGuire and R. F. C. Hull. Princeton: Princeton University Press, 1977.

_____. *The Collected Works of C. G. Jung*, 2d ed., vol. 7, *Two Essays on Analytical Psychology*. Princeton: Princeton University Press, 1975.

_____. *The Collected Works of C. G. Jung*, 2d ed., vol 8, *The Structure and Dynamics of the Psyche*. Princeton: Princeton University Press, 1969.

_____. *The Collected Works of C. G. Jung*, 2d ed., vol. 9ii, *The Archetypes and the Collective Unconscious*. Princeton: Princeton University Press, 1978.

_____. *The Collected Works of C. G. Jung*, 2d ed., vol 11, *Psychology and Religion: West and East*. Princeton: Princeton University Press, 1969.

_____. *Modern Man in Search of a Soul*. New York: Harcourt, Brace, Jovanovich, 1933.

_____. *The Portable Jung*. Translated by R. F. C. Hull, ed., Joseph Campbell. New York: The Viking Press, 1971.

_____. *The Undiscovered Self*. Translated by R. F. C. Hull. New York: Mentor Books, 1958.

Kierkegaard, Søren. *Purity of Heart is to Will One Thing*. New York: Harper & Row, 1956.

Lewis, C. S. *God in the Dock*. Grand Rapids: Wm. B. Eerdmans Publishing Co., 1970.

_____. *Mere Christianity*. New York: Macmillan Publishing Co., 1952.

_____. *That Hideous Strength*. New York: Macmillan Publishing Co., 1946.

Peck, M. Scott. *The Different Drum: Community Making and Peace*. New York: Simon & Schuster, 1987.

_____. *Further Along the Road Less Traveled*. New York: Simon & Schuster, 1993.

_____. *A World Waiting to be Born*. New York: Bantam Books, 1993.

Peterson, Eugene H. The Message: The New Testament in Contemporary English. Colorado Springs: NavPress, 1993.

_____. *Run With the Horses*. Downers Grove: InterVarsity Press, 1983.

_____. *Traveling Light: Reflections on the Free Life*. Downers Grove: InterVarsity Press, 1982.

Phillips, J. B. *The New Testament in Modern English*. London: Geoffrey Bles, 1963.

Sanford, John A. *The Invisible Partners*. Mahwah: Paulist Press, 1980.

_____. *The Strange Trial of Mr. Hyde*. New York: Harper & Row, 1987.

Stedman, Ray C. *Authentic Christianity*. Portland: Multnomah Press, 1975.

Stevenson, Robert Louis. *The Strange Case of Dr. Jekyll and Mr. Hyde*. New York: Puffin Books, 1985.

Solzhenitsyn, Aleksandr. *A World Split Apart*. New York: Harper & Row, 1978.

Tennyson, Alfred, Lord, "Sir Galahad" in *The Poems and Plays of Alfred Lord Tennyson*. New York: Random House, 1938.

Tozer, A. W. *That Incredible Christian*. Harrisburg: Christian Publications, Inc., 1948.

_____. *The Root of the Righteous*. Harrisburg: Christian Publications, Inc., 1955.

_____. *The Pursuit of God*. Harrisburg: Christian Publications, Inc., 1948.

Yankelovich, Daniel. *New Rules: Searching for Self-Fulfillment in a World Turned Upside Down*. New York: Random House, 1981.

INDEX

Give the Gift of
Shadow Work
to Your Friends and Colleagues
CHECK YOUR LEADING BOOKSTORE OR ORDER HERE

❏ **YES**, I want _____ copies of *Shadow Work* at $14.00 each (Tennessee residents please add $1.15 sales tax per book). Canadian orders must be accompanied by a postal money order in U.S. funds. Allow 15 days for delivery.

Shipping: $4.00 for the first book and
$2.00 per each additional book.

My check or money order for $_____ is enclosed.
Please charge my: ❏ Visa ❏ MasterCard
❏ American Express ❏ Discover

Name _____

Organization _____

Address _____

City/State/Zip _____

Phone _____

Card # _____ Exp. Date _____

Signature _____

Please make your check payable and return to:
Growth Solutions
PO Box 32805
Knoxville, TN 37930-2805

Call your credit card order to: (877) 671-1212
(Have your check information or credit card ready.)

You may also order by fax: (423) 675-6266
or e-mail: GrowthSol@aol.com